Legal Dimensions of Education

Implications for Teachers and School Administrators

Jerome G. Delaney

DETSELIG
ENTERPRISES LTD

Legal Dimensions of Education:
Implications for Teachers and School Administrators

Library and Archives Canada Cataloguing in Publication

Delaney, Jerome G.
Legal dimensions of education : implications for teachers and administrators / Jerome Delaney.

Includes bibliographical references.
ISBN 978-1-55059-314-3

1. Educational law and legislation – Canada. 2. Teachers – Legal status, laws, etc. – Canada. 3. School administrators – Legal status, laws, etc. – Canada. I. Title.

KE3805.D44 2007 344.71'07
C2007-904629-0
KF4119.D44 2007

Detselig Enterprises Ltd.

21, 1220 Kensington Road NW

Calgary, Alberta T2N 3P5

Phone: (403) 283-0900

Fax: (403) 283-6947

Email: temeron@telusplanet.net

www.temerondetselig.com

Support for our publishing program is recognized from the Government of Canada through the Book Publishing Industry Development Program (BPIDP).

Support is also acknowledged from the Alberta Foundation for the Arts for our publishing program.

Cover design by Alvin Choong

ISBN 978-1-55059-314-3   SAN 113-0234   Printed in Canada

To a wonderful friend and mentor,
Wayne William White
(1945 – 2004)

Preface

The Legal Dimensions of Education: Implications for Teachers and School Administrators attempts to give an overview of the various legal topics that are currently confronting teachers and school administrators in the K-12 school systems across Canada. Although by no means exhaustive, the list is one of considerable interest with references to decisions by the highest court in the land, the Supreme Court of Canada.

The Charter of Rights and Freedoms enacted in 1982 has now been with us for a quarter of a century. It is slowly but surely impacting on the way that teachers and school administrators go about their daily work with students and colleagues. Hopefully, Chapter 1 does justice to the Charter as it continues to evolve and develop in its application to education.

This handbook is designed to give teachers (preservice and practicing), and indeed the reader in general, a valuable introduction to and an overview of the legal aspects of education. The discussion questions at the end of each chapter should help to clarify the reader's own thinking on these various dimensions.

Acknowledgments

I wish to thank several individuals and groups who were most helpful in my efforts to bring this book to fruition:

The several students in my undergraduate course, Education 4420 (Legal and Moral Issues in Education) during these past several years who assisted me greatly in helping me to clarify my own thinking on these various topics; their insights and commentary were great motivators.

The several students in my graduate course, Education 6335 (The Legal Foundations of Educational Administration) during these past several years who also assisted me in the same way. Their various teaching experiences were particularly insightful and motivating.

Undergraduate students, Brad Jones and Neil Tremblett who offered constructive commentary on various sections.

My son, Colin who was always there to provide technical advice on formatting and other word processing matters.

My wife, Philomena for patiently tolerating my absences from home and for her unlimited understanding when a variety of domestic chores didn't get done!

To my colleagues in the Faculty of Education, Memorial University – Dr. Trudi Johnson, Dr. Dale Kirby, Dr. Dennis Mulcahy and Dr. Dennis Treslan for their insightful, helpful and encouraging comments on an earlier draft of this publication.

And lastly, to Dr. Ted Giles of Detselig for his patience and understanding in awaiting the final draft!

Contents

About the Author

Jerome G. Delaney is an assistant professor of educational administration in the Faculty of Education at Memorial University of Newfoundland. He holds a Doctor of Philosophy (PhD) in educational administration from the University of Alberta. Prior to joining the Faculty of Education, Dr. Delaney served as a high school teacher and a high school principal (3 principalships) throughout Newfoundland and Labrador.

His primary teaching and research interests are effective teaching, educational law and educational policy. His first book *Educational Policy Studies: A Practical Approach* was published by Detselig Enterprises Ltd. in 2002. He welcomes comments by email at jdelaney@mun.ca.

1

Introduction

It has been said that today we are living in a highly litigious society. Simply stated, it means that more so than ever before our citizenry is quite keen on their individual rights and are prepared to advocate for those rights. Technological advances with respect to the use of the internet and the media in general facilitate individuals becoming more informed as to what those rights are, thus affording them a degree of comfort in ensuring that their rights are protected and honored.

What does all of this mean for teachers and school administrators? Today's schoolhouse is a complex assortment of a multitude of individual persons and their accompanying dynamics gathered together in relatively close quarters. On a day to day basis, things happen in schools and little wonder that some of those happenings evoke and often necessitate legalized or quasi-legalized responses.

This legal context is one that teachers and school administrators live with every day and they are very often challenged as to how to deal with the various situations that arise on a consistently regular basis. There is a very real need for educators to have some understanding of the legal dimensions in which they operate.

Rationale for Studying Educational Law

Teachers completing a Bachelor of Education degree may or may not undertake a study of educational law in their respective university programs. In some programs across this country such a course is mandatory, whereas in the majority of cases, a course in educational law is optional. Students doing a graduate degree in educational leadership or educational administration are very seldom required to complete a course in educational law. This current state of affairs is problematic for several reasons:

1. If students on their way to becoming teachers do not study educational law prior to their entering the classroom, how will they become aware of their legal rights and responsibilities as practicing teachers? The answer suggested here is that such awareness will result from a reactionary stance mean-

ing that this awareness will come after the fact. Once something of a negative nature has happened in the classroom or school building at large, then and then only will the teacher or school administrator be compelled to consider the legal ramifications of one's action or lack of action. In any human activity, proaction as opposed to reaction is usually the preferred course of action. This is especially true of teaching and schooling.

2. Teachers in certain provinces (e.g., Ontario) are required to complete a course in Educational Law in order to qualify for their teaching certificate. Such a course is done under the purview of the Ontario College of Teachers. Not to diminish the value of having teachers complete this course for certification, Sydor (2006) points out that

> A minimalist interpretation of education law for teacher candidates enumerates and conceptualizes the law as a set of rules; this is sufficient for purposes of certification. Alternatively, the acts and regulations respecting education can be understood along with common law as the narrative framework for hope about how we might organize our social relationships with respect to the institution of education. The first approach permits an organized and orderly operation of our schools; the second makes transformation beyond order possible. (p. 930)

One would suggest that in a university class students under the facilitation of a qualified instructor have the opportunity for a much broader discussion and engagement of the various issues experienced by educators in schools. The law at first blush appears to be black and white but upon closer scrutiny one realizes that this is not always the case; context plays a very valuable role in legal interpretations.

3. By the very nature of graduate programs in educational leadership or educational administration, students are encouraged and sometimes required to have a certain amount of teaching experience prior to entering the program. In educational law classes this allows for richer class discussions and hopefully results in a greater understanding of and appreciation for the value of being informed on the various laws relevant to education. Teachers going on to serve in leadership positions either at the school building or district levels will be called upon to proffer advice and guidance to their colleagues. It is imperative that they have an informed knowledge base of educational law. One could say that faculties of education offering graduate programs in educational leadership or educational administration are negligent in not requiring their students to study educational law!

Law and Educational Administration

A major aspect of educational administration in the K-12 school system is dealing with conflicts, whether they be student-student, student-teacher,

teacher-administration, parent-teacher, parent-administration, or school administration-school board. The law is utilized as one of the major problem-solving mechanisms in educational administration and so it behooves those in administration to have an adequate working knowledge of "all things legal in school administration." *The Charter of Rights and Freedoms,* provincial school or education acts, teacher collective agreements, due process, grievance and arbitration procedures, liability and negligence are but a few of the topics that school administrators will become familiar with in their routine work in schools.

Richter (1994) offers this insight into the role that law plays in the practice of educational administration:

> From a broad perspective administration can be looked at as a decision-making process in organizations in which law has a dual function:

> The decision-making process itself must be organized. Who is to decide what, and how are decisions to be made? The law determines competencies and procedures.

> Decision making in organizations is a very complex process. What are the organization's aims and by what means can they be reached? Law restricts the free choice of aims and means. (p. 3272)

Educational law is certainly no panacea for solving all the problems and challenges that teachers and school administrators will experience in their everyday work with the various stakeholders. But as suggested above by Richter, it does have the potential to provide a framework for dealing with those problems and challenges.

Conclusion

Educational law has a positive and practical role to play in the daily work of educators. For educators to be effective in their various roles, it is imperative that they be cognizant of and conversant with the numerous legal dimensions of their profession. The study of educational law is an ongoing affair due to the changing nature of society's expectations for education and schooling.

For Discussion

1. What are the common everyday perceptions of educational law that prevail in schools in general and staffrooms in particular ?

2 If you were to select two to three high priority topics to study in educational law, what would they be and why?

3. Do you think that teachers and school administrators perceive educational law (or the legal dimensions of education) to be a significant part of their work as educators? Elaborate.

4. Primary-elementary v. junior-senior high sectors of schools: Does either one of these sectors call for a greater understanding of the legal dimensions of education? Elaborate.

2

The Charter of Rights and Freedoms

The Canada Act 1982 came into effect on April 17, 1982 and marked a very significant milestone in our country's history, that of patriation of Canada's constitution. A country's constitution provides a framework from which the country operates and with this patriation, Canada became totally independent from the mother country, Britain.

Although the *Canada Act* is divided into several parts, the section that has the most legal significance for educators is Part 1, the *Canadian Charter of Rights and Freedoms*. A copy of the Charter is included in this publication as Appendix A.

Role of the Judiciary

Prior to the enactment of the Charter in 1982, the courts were primarily preoccupied with issues stemming from the interpretation of statutes (provincial or federal laws) that impacted on education. Most of the time judges respected the day to day decision-making of educators and left the running of schools up to the teachers and administrators. This has often been referred to as "judicial deference" meaning that the judiciary very often respected and went along with those decisions made by educators because it was the thinking of the judiciary that it was those educators who were trained to run the schools and it was they who had the legislative authority to do so.

However, after the enactment of the Charter, the role of the judiciary changed significantly. Although judges continued to interpret laws in order to determine if they had been broken, they were now charged with the task of judging the laws of the land (Black-Branch, 1997). This was quite a change from the status quo and placed what could be termed as an onerous responsibility on the judiciary.

In the words of Black-Branch (1997):

The Charter grants judges the power to scrutinize laws to ensure compliance with these rights. Chief Justice Antonio Lamer, in an interview commemorating the tenth anniversary of the *Charter of Rights and Freedoms* (in 1992), stated that there is no doubt the courts have seized a wider role

17

in scrutinizing laws. In the article, "How the Charter changes justice" [*Globe and Mail*, April 17, 1992] Chief Justice Lamer stated "not only to this court [the Supreme Court of Canada], but all courts and judges, the Charter has changed our job descriptions . . . with the Charter we are commanded . . . to sometimes judge the laws themselves." (pp. 21-22)

Applicability of the Charter

Educators should note that the Charter has application to schools and as Watkinson (1999) states,

... the Charter's net falls over the actions, policies, and decisions of departments of education, school boards, and school administrators, as well as over curricula and pedagogical theories. The Supreme Court has also made it clear that independent or private schools that exercise delegated governmental power or are otherwise responsible for the implementation of government policy, such as providing a public education, are bound by the Charter. The rationale, the Court said, is obvious: "Governments should not be permitted to evade their Charter responsibilities by implementing policy through the vehicle of private arrangements." (p. 27)

The Concept of Reasonableness

Permeating the thinking behind the Charter is the concept of reasonableness. On a first reading of the various sections of the Charter, teachers and school administrators may become somewhat concerned and perhaps even paranoid when they come upon sections titled freedom of speech, freedom of assembly, freedom of association and freedom of opinion and expression. However, in Section 1 of the Charter it is acknowledged that the concept of reasonableness must prevail; nothing is absolute. The specific section reads:

The Canadian Charter of Rights and Freedoms guarantees the rights and freedoms set out in it subject only to such reasonable limits prescribed by law as can be demonstrably justified in a free and democratic society.

It is indeed acknowledged that limitations may from time to time be placed on rights and freedoms in order to promote a broader social "good" within the Canadian community (Black-Branch, 1997). Black-Branch (1997) goes on to say that

This limitations clause was deemed necessary by politicians at the time of enacting the Charter in order to curtail abuses of rights and freedoms by extremist individuals using their rights to work against the perceived "good" of society. Its purpose is to protect the community against potentially divisive and negative consequences which stem from the absolute exercise of rights and freedoms. For example, a person promoting hatred against a certain class of people may ultimately be denied his or her freedom of speech. As a result, freedom of speech is not absolute, it does have limits. (p. 24)

Obviously, the same can be said of the happenings and day to day occurrences in schools. For obvious reasons, schools operate with a multitude of rules and regulations to ensure the efficient and orderly running of the educational establishment. There are times when students are involved in disruptive and unacceptable behaviors in the classroom and around the school. In fact, such negative behaviors are not only confined to students but rather could also involve various other educational personnel (i.e., teachers and support staff such as secretaries, student assistants, maintenance and janitorial staff).

Individual school policies (e.g., student discipline policies), teachers' codes of ethics, teacher collective agreements, education acts, and school board policies are all examples of laws that impact on behaviors in the school setting. As long as these various laws demonstrate that they are reasonable and necessary for the efficient running of schools on a day to day basis, the courts should not have a problem with respect to their conforming to Section 1 of the Charter.

Relevance to Education

There are a number of sections in the Charter that have direct relevance to the work of teachers and administrators. Specifically, they are:

Section 1: Guarantee of Rights and Freedoms

Section 2: Fundamental Freedoms

Sections 7 - 12: Legal Rights

Section 15: Equality Rights

Section 23: Minority Language Educational Rights

Section 24: Enforcement

Consideration of the significance of each of these sections to education will now be discussed.

Guarantee of Rights and Freedoms – Section 1

Section 1 reads as follows:

The *Canadian Charter of Rights and Freedoms* guarantees the rights and freedoms set out in it subject only to such reasonable limits prescribed by law as can be demonstrably justified in a free and democratic society.

Under this section the courts can either uphold or strike down an action based on whether or not a limitation is reasonable and demonstrably justified in a free and democratic society (Brown & Zuker, 2002). According to Watkinson (1999), the importance of this section should not be underestimated. She goes on to say that

> Every Charter analysis involves a two-stage process. First, the courts must decide whether a challenged law limits a guaranteed right. At this stage the onus of proving that an alleged breach of the Charter has occurred due to the actions of the government or its agent is placed upon the individual challenging the law or government action. If the court agrees that the challenged law limits a guaranteed right, it moves to the second stage, which is to determine whether the limit upon the right can be justified under section 1. The onus of proof shifts to the government or its agent seeking to uphold the limitation. The government or its agent must show that the limit is a reasonable one and can be [as the Charter states] demonstrably justified in a free and democratic society. (p. 25)

In the school system consider the situation when a student directs a profanity at a teacher and is appropriately disciplined. Does the student have protection from this discipline as a result of the freedom of expression clause in Section 2(b) of the Charter? One would suggest that in the school system there is a reasonable limit placed on students' right to freedom of expression and hence the school's right to discipline students for such unacceptable behavior.

Depending on the nature of the student's profanity in this particular case, such discipline may result in a suspension from school. However, if the school administration decided to initiate expulsion proceedings for this unacceptable behavior, one could justifiably argue whether or not this would be a reasonable course of action to take. In other words, is it reasonable and justifiable in a free and democratic society? Common sense should dictate that the punishment fit the crime and expulsion would obviously suggest that this is "overkill" and certainly not reasonable and justifiable.

Fundamental Freedoms – Section 2

This section states:

a. Everyone has the following fundamental freedoms:

b. freedom of conscience and religion;

c. freedom of thought, belief, opinion and expression, including freedom of the press and other media of communication;

d. freedom of peaceful assembly; and

e. freedom of association.

Because of the nature of schools, these freedoms take on a particular significance when it comes to the enforcement of rules and regulations on a daily basis. Consider for example freedom of opinion. A female student is involved in spreading malicious rumors about another female student resulting in a parent coming into the building to speak to the school administration about the stress that these rumors are causing the affected student. Again, freedom of expression in the school and society at large does not mean that a person has carte blanche to say whatever he or she feels like saying especially when it comes to the point of being malicious and hurtful.

As alluded to earlier, the concept of reasonableness has to prevail and the students in the school setting would be at considerable risk if such reasonableness were not enforced from a disciplinary perspective. The other freedoms in this section should be interpreted in the same manner.

The freedom of religion clause is one that has received some attention in the courts across Canada. Hurlbert and Hurlbert (1992) have this to say:

> Most provincial statutes presently provide for some form of religious exercise, with exculpation if written parental consent is given. A recent Ontario Court of Appeal case found that this sort of legislative provision is unconstitutional. Although Ontario's highest court struck down a provincial regulation compelling school boards to open or close each school day with religious exercises, the ratio for the decision indicates that religious exercises should not be conducted in any public school in Canada – whether provincial statutes/regulations make them mandatory (as in Manitoba and British Columbia); whether local school boards provide for them under permissive legislation (as in Saskatchewan and Alberta); or whether teachers conduct them on their own initiative (as in New Brunswick). However, the issue has yet to be decided by the Supreme Court of Canada. (pp. 179-180)

Legal Rights

Legal rights are covered in Sections 7 to 12. In the past teachers and school administrators have enjoyed considerable latitude and autonomy when it came to the enforcement of school rules and regulations. Although parents did not always agree with the decisions of administrators regarding disciplinary actions taken against their sons and daughters, such disagreements seldom ended up in the courts. However, under the Charter such disciplinary actions come under a much greater scrutiny and parents now have the right to petition courts should they believe their children have been unfairly treated. Prior to the advent of the Charter, courts paid judicial deference to the decisions of school administrators:

> The traditional approach of Canadian courts to the matter of students' procedural rights in school discipline cases has been to defer almost com-

pletely to school officials' discretion and to prefer the virtues of discipline and obedience over those associated with individual rights and challenging authority. (Dickinson & MacKay, 1989, p. 318)

Section 7

Section 7 of the Charter reads:

Everyone has the right to life, liberty and security of the person and the right not to be deprived thereof except in accordance with the principles of fundamental justice.

According to the *Canadian Law Dictionary* (Yogis, 1995), natural [fundamental] justice is defined as ." . . [giving] persons specifically affected by the decision a reasonable opportunity of presenting their case, [being listened] to fairly and [having a decision reached] untainted by bias" (p. 152). Young and Levin (2002) have expressed concerns with respect to students' being denied natural justice in the enforcement of school disciplinary policies:

School discipline practices frequently appear to violate principles of natural justice. For example, teachers often accuse students of misdemeanours and impose punishments on them without explaining precisely what the transgression is and without providing an opportunity for the students' position to be heard. In effect, students may be compelled to give evidence against themselves (prohibited under Section 11c). Students are not always presumed innocent until proven guilty by a public and impartial tribunal (Section 11d). Appeal processes may not exist, and so on. (p. 117)

In the everyday life of schools disciplinary infractions by students and their subsequent referrals to the "principal's office" can be many and one has to temper the practicalities of student discipline policies with the overall intent of the legal rights section of the Charter. The following advice is offered to teachers and administrators when dealing with disciplinary issues:

1. At all times students should be accorded dignity and respect when being dealt with.

2. Students, depending on the nature and severity of the infraction, should be afforded a reasonable degree of privacy and confidentiality in the resulting discussions.

3. Apprise students of the "problem" that is being confronted.

4. Give students the opportunity to present "their side of the story."

5. Inform students of any decisions reached by the teacher/administrator and the rationale behind the particular decision.

6. Advise parent(s) of the situation and of any decisions reached with respect to detentions and/or suspensions. Of course, depending on the severity or gravity of the situation, the teacher/administrator will have to make a decision as to whether or not parent(s) should be informed.

7. Give the parent(s) the opportunity to present an appeal. Schools should have an appropriate appeal procedure in place.

One cannot overemphasize the importance of students being given due process or procedural fairness. It is not only important that justice be given but that it be perceived that justice has been given. In the past teachers and administrators may have resorted to shouting and yelling at students, very often demeaning them. In today's society such tactics are highly offensive and in considerable contrast to and violation of the principles of natural justice referred to in Section 7 of the Charter.

Consider the following case (cited in Watkinson, 1999):

> A 1984 Charter case decided by the Newfoundland District Court ruled in favor of a teacher who wished to teach his ten-year-old daughter at home. .... this case did not revolve around freedom of religion, but rather the parent's right under section 7. The teacher argued that section 7 gives parents the right to make certain decisions about their children and the right cannot be taken away without at least affording "the principle of fundamental justice" envisaged in section 7 of the Charter. The court ruled that the superintendent's refusal to approve the parent's program of instruction, which was based on a program obtained from the Manitoba Department of Education, violated the principles of fundamental justice because the parent had no right of hearing, appeal or review. (p. 70)

Section 8

This section states that "Everyone has the right to be secure against unreasonable search or seizure." This section is of particular significance to teachers and school administrators because there are situations which necessitate the searching of students' belongings and lockers. From time to time items of value are stolen in schools, and drugs and other illegal paraphernalia are brought into school buildings jeopardizing the safety and security of all those who are housed in those buildings.

According to Watkinson (1999), the central issue around this section is the balance between the constitutional right to be secure from unreasonable search and seizure and the legal obligation for school officials to provide safe and secure educational environments. Adding to the complexity of the issue is whether or not

. . . school officials when conducting a search of a student, that is, whether they are acting *in loco parentis* (in the place of the parent) or as agents of the state; and the legality of strip searches, locker searches, and the search of personal property. (p. 151)

The Supreme Court of Canada has ruled that the standard to be applied to searches by school authorities depends on whether or not the school authorities were acting as agents of the police (Brown & Zuker, 2002). Brown and Zuker go on to state:

If the school authorities are acting as agents of the police, they must meet the same standards as the police in order to engage in a search. However, if they are not agents of the police, a different standard is applied. (p. 219)

The following advice with respect to the approach to be taken when searching students is offered as a result of the R. v. M. (M.R.) appeal to the Supreme Court of Canada in 1998:

1. A warrant is not essential in order to conduct a search of a student by a school authority.

2. The school authority must have reasonable grounds to believe that there has been a breach of school regulations or discipline and that a search of a student would reveal evidence of that breach.

3. School authorities will be in the best position to assess information given to them and relate it to the situation in their schools.

4. The following may constitute reasonable grounds in this context: information received from one student considered to be credible, information received from more than one student, a teacher's or principal's own observations, or any combination of these pieces of information which the relevant authority considers to be credible. The compelling nature of the information and the credibility of these or other sources must be assessed by the school authority in the context of these circumstances existing at the particular school.(www.canlii.org/ca/cas/scc/1998/1998scc84.html p. 4)

The Supreme Court of Canada further stated that the following factors should be considered when determining whether a search conducted by a teacher or principal in the school environment was reasonable:

1. The first step is to determine whether it can be inferred from the provisions of the relevant Education Act that teachers and principals are authorized to conduct searches of their students in appropriate circumstances. In the school environment such a statutory authorization would be reasonable.

2. The search itself must be carried out in a reasonable manner. It should be conducted in a sensitive manner and be minimally intrusive.

3. In order to determine whether a search was reasonable, all the surrounding circumstances will have to be considered. (www.canlii.org/ca-/cas/scc/1998/1998scc84.html p. 4)

A further caution is added by the Supreme Court of Canada:

This modified standard for reasonable searches should apply to searches of students on school property conducted by teachers or school officials within the scope of their responsibility and authority to maintain order, discipline and safety within the school. This standard will not apply to any actions taken which are beyond the scope of the authority of teachers or principals. Further, a different situation arises if the school authorities are acting as agents of the police where the normal standards will apply. (www.canlii.org/ca/cas/scc/1998/1998scc84.html pp. 4-5)

Section 9

"Everyone has the right not to be arbitrarily detained or imprisoned."

In the everyday lives of students when they breach school rules and regulations detention is commonplace. Section 9 of the Charter only applies to students in criminal matters; it does not apply to students being detained by teachers and administrators for infractions of school rules and regulations.

However, the following advice is offered teachers and administrators when assigning detentions to students:

1. Give students a minimum of one day's notice that s/he has to serve a detention. By detention is meant having to spend time with the teacher/administrator during lunchtime or after school.

2. With respect to lunchtime detentions, however, students should be given a reasonable period of time to eat their lunch.

3. The amount of time for the detention should again be reasonable and in the case of junior high students (Grades 7, 8, 9), it is recommended that the teacher/administrator notify the parent directly of the time of the detention and the reason for it. Given the age and maturity of senior high students (Grades 10, 11, 12), there is probably no need to contact the parents; advise students that they are responsible for telling their parents.

4. Students serving detention should be supervised by the teacher/administrator at all times.

Section 10

This section reads as follows:

Everyone has the right on arrest or detention

a. to be informed promptly of the reasons thereof;

b. to retain and instruct counsel without delay and to be informed of that right; and

c. to have the validity of the detention determined by way of *habeas corpus* and to be released if the detention is not lawful.

Although this section only applies to students involved in criminal matters, teachers and administrators do have an ethical responsibility to ensure that students are informed very explicitly of the reason(s) for their being assigned a detention(s). And depending on the specific circumstances, teachers and administrators should keep parents apprised of situations when their sons and daughters run afoul of school rules and regulations.

Understandably so, students do not always tell their parents what is happening in school and even more so, when they end up in the principal's office for unacceptable behavior. Also, when they do tell their parents, they present their side of the story and this often places school officials at a disadvantage as parents, at first blush, tend to side with their children. However, after parents have been informed of the school's perspectives on the matter at hand, they for the most part are very supportive of the school's efforts to correct the problem. The value of communication between the home and the school can never be underestimated.

Section 11

This section of the Charter lists the various rights a person has after having being charged with an offence (refer to Appendix A for the actual text of Section 11). Although this section does not have direct relevance to the everyday work of teachers and administrators, it can offer us some salient advice in dealing with school matters of an investigative nature. The first two rights listed in this section refer to being informed without unreasonable delay of the specific offence and to be tried within a reasonable time.

Although rather obvious, it is incumbent upon teachers and administrators to deal with student disciplinary matters as expeditiously as possible. A significant delay in taking action tends to result in a downgrading or downplaying of the gravity of the specific incident and in the hustle and bustle of everyday school life, other demands come up fairly quickly, sometimes resulting in the original matter being "lost" or forgotten. In the case of a referral to the principal's or vice-principal's office, this can often leave the referring teacher with a sense of not being supported by the school administration and with the student who has been referred, a feeling that s/he has "dodged the bullet" this time. Other students are quick to pick up on this lack of appropriate action from the general office and so a message, subtle though it be, is perceived by students throughout the school that disciplinary matters of this nature sometimes or perhaps often, get overlooked.

Section 12

This section reads as follows:

Everyone has the right not to be subjected to any cruel and unusual treatment or punishment.

Although we tend to think of infliction of physical pain when we hear the terms "cruel and unusual treatment or punishment," such is not always the case in fact. Students are sometimes subjected to ridicule, degradation and extreme sarcasm in the classroom and in administrative offices by insensitive and uncaring teachers and administrators. One would hope that these situations are in the minority but the reality is that although most unfortunate, they do happen. Students, no matter what age, are very vulnerable and the impact we as educators have on their development is indeed mind-boggling. It is therefore imperative on us as their educators to treat them fairly and with the dignity and respect that we, ourselves, would expect if we were those students.

We can all remember very negative student-teacher experiences that we either experienced personally or observed being experienced by other students and these experiences were very difficult emotionally. Granted, the craft of teaching does present us educators with a multitude of challenges on a daily basis; however, we are the ones who have received a minimum of four to five years of university preparation to become teachers and we are the adults. The expectation is that we have to take the high road and not resort to the level of some of our students who are immature and lacking in the finer graces of appropriate behavior on a consistent basis. This is many times easier said than done, but nevertheless that is the expectation of us as teachers and administrators.

Most provincial education acts or statutes in Canada prohibit the use of corporal punishment. However, in a recent ruling by the Supreme Court of Canada, Section 43 of the *Criminal Code of Canada* which does condone the use of corporal punishment was further clarified to mean that teachers could only use physical force to restrain a student such as when breaking up a fight. Chapter 7 on corporal punishment will discuss this issue in much greater detail.

Equality Rights

Section 15

This section reads as follows:

1. Every individual is equal before and under the law and has the right to the equal protection and equal benefit of the law without discrimination and, in particular, without discrimination based on race, national or ethnic origin, colour, religion, sex, age or mental or physical disability.

2. Subsection (1) does not preclude any law, program or activity that has as its object the amelioration of conditions of disadvantaged individuals or groups including those that are disadvantaged because of race, national or ethnic origin, colour, religion, sex, age or mental or physical disability.

This section has direct relevance to education, specifically to the area of special education. According to Brown and Zuker (2002),

Exceptional children are entitled to special education programs and services to which other children are not entitled. For instance, they may be provided with a one-on-one instructional assistant throughout the school day. The law provides them with specific entitlements because treating people equally does not always result in equality. Some pupils must be treated differently in order to have equality. (p. 296)

Section 23

This section of the Charter deals with minority language educational rights (refer to Appendix A for the actual text). It contains significant guarantees of minority language rights. There are three main criteria that determine the rights of Canadian citizens of the English and French-speaking minorities in each province to have their children educated in their own language:

1. Mother tongue. If your mother tongue (first language learned and still understood) is French and you live in a mainly English-speaking province, you will have a constitutional right to have your children educated in French. This criterion is of vital importance to French-speaking Canadians outside Quebec as it insures that French Canadian children have access to an education in French, even if their parents did not receive instruction in French.

2. Language in which the parents were educated in Canada. If you were educated in English in Canada and you live in Quebec, you can send your children to school in English in that province. Similarly, if you were educated in French in Canada and live in one of the other nine provinces, you can have your children educated in French in those provinces.

3. Language in which other children in the family are receiving or have received their education. If you have one child who has received primary or secondary school instruction in English or French in Canada, you have the right to have all your children educated in the same language. (Canadian Unity Information Office, 1984, pp. 22-24)

Common sense dictates of course that these three criteria depend on there being a sufficient number of children eligible for minority language education in an area to warrant setting up schools in that language for them out of public funds.

Criteria two and three – language in which parents and other children were educated – apply with respect to the minority language education systems (either French or English) in all 10 provinces. Meeting either one of these criteria means a constitutional guarantee of access to minority language education systems across Canada.

Criterion one – access by virtue of mother tongue – applies in all provinces except Quebec.

Section 24

This section refers to the actual enforcement of the rights and freedoms that are guaranteed in the Charter (see Appendix A for the actual text). Persons or groups who feel that they have had their rights and freedoms denied or infringed upon may apply to a court for a remedy deemed appropriate and just in the circumstances. The following examples are illustrations of how this enforcement provision might work in actual practice:

> If some public servant should attempt to prevent your group from religious worship, you would be able to apply for a restraining order and sue for damages, if any. If you were an accused person and denied bail without just cause, you would be able to apply to another court for a bail order. If the police were to break into and search your premises illegally and find evidence of a crime, the courts could exclude such evidence in a subsequent trial in which it is alleged that a right under the Charter has been infringed, and if the Court finds that the admission of such evidence would bring the administration of justice into disrepute. This power to exclude evidence in limited circumstances will permit the courts to preserve public respect for the integrity of the judicial process. (Canadian Unity Information Office, 1984, p. 26)

Conclusion

The Charter of Rights and Freedoms has transformed how we look at educational matters from a legalistic perspective. In pre-Charter days, the rights of students and parents were simply not a part of the discourse. Today, all matters of education dealing with students and parents are subject to the scrutiny of the Charter. Because of the Charter's national scope, a decision involving a student being deprived of his/her rights to due process in the province of Nova Scotia will have implications for students in British Columbia. This "nationalizing influence" of the Charter (MacKay &

Sutherland, 1992) is a positive development in education because it ensures a certain degree of uniformity and consistency for students.

According to MacKay and Sutherland (1992), "the Charter has altered the educational landscape in two significant ways."

> First, it provides parents with a tool for challenging the substance of school board decisions. Before the Charter, parents were restricted to administrative law remedies that dealt primarily with procedural irregularities. The broad discretion enjoyed by school boards in delivering educational services prior to the Charter is now being eroded.

> Second, the Charter has national scope. The Charter is the supreme law of Canada and applies to all Canadians. Decisions of the Supreme Court of Canada are binding on all provinces. Therefore, if a Charter issue in education makes its way to the Supreme Court of Canada, the decision of that court will apply to every province whether or not a particular province had any part in the case. (pp. 37-38)

In sum, teachers and administrators should be aware of the various sections of the *Charter of Rights and Freedoms* so that they can use common sense and reasonableness when they interact with students and the various players in education on a daily basis. The concept of reasonableness, as alluded to previously, continues to be a major criterion in the determination of court cases as they relate to educational matters. Nothing to date with respect to cases involving the principles articulated in the Charter suggests otherwise.

For Discussion

1. What are the various perceptions, if any, of the *Charter of Rights and Freedoms* prevalent in today's schools? Are these accurate perceptions? Discuss.

2. Permeating the Charter is the concept of reasonableness. Has the concept of reasonableness in our schools increased in recent years solely because of the Charter or are there other factors in today's society which have contributed to this increased emphasis? Discuss.

3. The rights of the individual versus the rights of the collective – discuss this concept in the light of classroom management and disruptive students.

3

Provincial Education Acts

Under Section 93 of the *BNA Act* (retitled the *Constitution Act, 1867* by the *Constitution Act, 1982*) responsibility for primary, elementary and secondary education in Canada lies with the governments of each province in Canada. This is operationalized by each province setting up a department or ministry of education with an elected member of the government serving as the head or minister of the department. All officials working under the minister are paid civil servants and they take their directives from the minister who in turn takes his/her direction from the elected government of the day.

Each province in Canada has an education or schools act which in general terms sets out the various expectations of schools and school boards and of the teachers and administrators who manage those schools and school boards. The sections or articles in these school/education acts are approved by the provincial legislatures and from time to time relevant sections are updated or amended which must also be approved by the provincial legislatures. Accompanying each education or school act is a set of regulations which provide additional, practical information supplementing the various sections of the specific act.

Although each province has its own distinct and separate schools/education act, a comparison of these statutes/laws from one end of the country to the other will show considerable similarities and few differences. Each education/school act will usually include sections on the following: students; teachers, administrators, parents; schools; school councils, and school boards. These sections are further broken down into subsections. For example, a section on students might deal with the following: conduct of students; right of access and attendance; and home instruction, to mention a few (*Newfoundland and Labrador Schools Act, 1997*).

A survey of the provincial education/school acts across the Canada reveals a number of common sections particularly relevant to the work of teachers and administrators. A discussion of these common sections now follows.

Students

Conduct

The Schools Act of Newfoundland and Labrador (1997) devotes a rather succinct but all encompassing statement in Section 11 on the conduct of students:

> Every student shall comply with school discipline and the rules of the school and shall carry out the learning activities within the prescribed curriculum.

The Saskatchewan Education Act (1995) goes into greater detail regarding the expectations of students:

Every pupil shall:

a. attend school regularly and punctually;

b. purchase any school supplies and materials not furnished by the board of education or the conseil scolaire that the principal considers necessary for [a] particular course of instruction;

c. observe standards approved by the board of education or the conseil scolaire with respect to (i) cleanliness and tidiness of person; (ii) general deportment; (iii) obedience; (iv) courtesy; and (v) the rights of other persons;

d. be diligent in his or her studies;

e. conform to the rules of the school approved by the board of education or the conseil scolaire and the conseil d'ecole; and

f. submit to any discipline that would be exercised by a kind, firm and judicious parent. (Section 150, subsection 3)

Section 151 further states that:

1. Every pupil is accountable to the teacher for the pupil's conduct on the school premises during school hours and during those hours that the teacher is in charge of the pupil or class or while engaged in authorized school activities conducted during out-of-school hours.

2. Every pupil is accountable to the principal for the pupil's general deportment at any time the pupil is under the supervision of the school and members of the teaching staff, including time spent in travelling between the school and the pupil's place of residence.

Part 6, section 72 of the *Prince Edward Island School Act* (1988) also speaks to student responsibilities:

Students enrolled in a school have the following responsibilities:

a. to observe the code of conduct and other rules and policies of the school board and of the school;

b. to attend classes regularly and punctually and participate in the educational programs in which the student is enrolled;

c. to be diligent in pursuing the student's studies;

d. to respect the rights of others.

Section 73 of the act focuses specifically on the discipline of students:

The manner in which a student is disciplined while attending school or school-sponsored activities shall be similar to that administered by a kind, firm and judicious parent but shall not include corporal punishment.

Similarly, the *Alberta School Act* (2000) states in Section 12:

A student shall conduct himself or herself so as to reasonably comply with the following code of conduct:

a. be diligent in pursuing the student's studies;

b. attend school regularly and punctually;

c. co-operate fully with everyone authorized by the board to provide education programs and other services;

d. comply with the rules of the school;

e. account to the student's teachers for the student's conduct;

f. respect the rights of others.

The above examples of specific statements related to student expectations for behavior and general deportment while attending school are typical of what is contained in all provincial schools/education acts across Canada. Note the commonality of the intent of the various words and phrases used: comply, obedience, courtesy, diligence, respect the rights of others, attending school regularly and punctually. Stated bluntly, students in schools across Canada have a statutory or legal duty to conduct themselves appropriately and to apply themselves diligently to their studies.

Right of Access and Attendance

The right to attend school is universal across Canada. Generally speaking, the age limitations range from 6 years to that of 21 years with some exceptions. Compulsory schooling begins at the age of six but in many provinces there is a non-compulsory kindergarten program for students who turn five by the end of December of that school year. Students are usually compelled to attend school until they reach the age of 16 years; however in most provinces students may legally remain in school until they turn 21 years of age.

Home Instruction

Home instruction or home schooling refers to exactly that – parents educating their sons and daughters at home. Most provincial legislation in Canada allows for this type of instruction "as long as the education provided is approximately equivalent to the standard found in the public schools" (Young & Levin, 2002, p. 130).

The *Ontario Education Act* (1990) states in Section 21(2) that "A child is excused from attendance at school if, (a) the child is receiving satisfactory instruction at home or elsewhere. . . "

Being somewhat more prescriptive, the province of Alberta in its *School Act* (2000) states in Section 29(1): "A parent of a student may provide, at home or elsewhere, a home education program for the student if the program (a) meets the requirements of the regulations, and (b) is under the supervision of a board or a private school accredited under section 28(2) [of this act].

Nova Scotia in its *Education Act* (1996) allows for the provision of home education under certain conditions. Section 128 states:

1. A parent may provide a home education program to a child of the parent centred in the child's home.

2. A parent providing a home education program to a child shall (a) register the child for each academic year with the Minister; and (b) report the child's progress to the Minister, as prescribed by the regulations.

3. With the approval of the school board, a child in a home education program may attend courses offered by the school board, subject to any terms and conditions prescribed by the school board.

The latest statistic available from Statistics Canada on the current number of students being home-schooled in Canada is 17 500, a significant increase over the past several years (Publication 81-003, 1997). Teachers and administrators may be called upon by school boards to provide assistance to parents who are home-schooling their children. How much assistance school boards could ask of teachers and administrators is not at all clear and is not addressed in the provincial legislation. Indications are that the number of students involved in home-schooling in this country will continue to grow in the years ahead.

Teachers

Every provincial education/schools statute devotes a section specifying the various expectations of teachers. Written somewhat idealistically, the wording is very similar across Canada. Consider these examples.

Section 27(1) of T*he New Brunswick Education Act* (1997) states:

The duties of a teacher employed in a school include

a. implementing the prescribed curriculum,

b. identifying and implementing learning and evaluation strategies that foster a positive learning environment aimed at helping each pupil achieve prescribed learning outcomes,

c. maintaining a deportment consistent with his or her position of trust and influence over young people,

d. exemplifying and encouraging in each pupil the values of truth, justice, compassion and respect for all persons,

e. attending to the health and well-being of each pupil,

f. maintaining his or her professional competence, and

g. assisting the development and implementation of the school improvement plan and co-operating in the preparation of the school performance report.

Section 27(2) adds that

A teacher employed in a school is accountable to the superintendent of the school district through the principal of the school for the performance of the teacher's duties and the overall educational progress of the pupils under the teacher's instruction.

The province of Alberta lists the expectations of teachers in its *School Act* (2000) in Section 18(1) & (2):

1. A teacher while providing instruction or supervision must

a. provide instruction competently to students;

b. teach the courses of study and education programs that are prescribed, approved or authorized pursuant to this Act;

c. promote goals and standards applicable to the provisions of education adopted or approved pursuant to this Act;

d. encourage and foster learning in students;

e. regularly evaluate students and periodically report the results of the evaluation to students, the students' parents and the board;

f. maintain, under the direction of the principal, order and discipline among the students while they are in the school or on the school grounds and while they are attending or participating in activities sponsored or approved by the board;

g. subject to any applicable collective agreement and the teacher's contract of employment, carry out those duties that are assigned by the principal or the board.

2. At any time during the period of time that a teacher is under an obligation to the board to provide instruction or supervision or to carry out duties assigned to the teacher by a principal or the board, a teacher must, at the request of the board,

a. participate in curriculum development and field testing of new curriculum;

b. develop, field test and mark provincial achievement tests and diploma examinations;

c. supervise student teachers.

The Quebec Education Act (2005) stipulates what it expects of teachers in Section 22 under the heading of "Teacher Obligations":

A teacher shall

1. contribute to the intellectual and overall personal development of each student entrusted to his care;

2. take part in instilling into each student entrusted to his care a desire to learn;

3. take the appropriate means to foster respect for human rights in his students;

4. act in a just and impartial manner in his dealings with his students;

5. take the necessary measures to promote the quality of written and spoken language;

6. take the appropriate measures to attain and maintain a high level of professionalism;

6.1 collaborate in the training of future teachers and in the mentoring of newly qualified teachers;

7. comply with the educational project of the school.

In this sample of education legislation it is significant to note that four themes permeate teacher expectations: teaching of the prescribed curriculum; accountability; maintenance of order and discipline; and teacher professionalism. This is common throughout all the provincial education legislation. In recent years accountability has become a catchword in education and coupled with accountability is the increased emphasis on standardized testing, both internal and external. According to McEwen (1995), provinces have increased substantially the amount of provincial testing, and the results are being used more publicly to evaluate the overall quality of the school system. The province of Alberta appears to be at the forefront of this recent emphasis on standardized testing and this emphasis is obvious with direct reference to provincial achievement tests in the section alluded to above.

Principals

The role of principals receives substantial attention in schools/education acts across Canada. This is not surprising as the principal is touted as the instructional leader and a major player in the education of students (Fullan, 2001; Hoy & Miskel, 2001; Sergiovanni, 1995; Young & Levin, 2002).

In Sections 24(3) the *Newfoundland and Labrador Schools Act* (1997) sets forth that province's expectations of its school principals:

A principal of a school shall, subject to the direction of the board,

a. provide instructional leadership in the school;

b. ensure that the instruction provided by the teachers employed in the school is consistent with the courses of study and education prescribed or approved under this Act;

c. ensure that the evaluation and grading of students is conducted in accordance with generally accepted standards in education;

d. evaluate or provide for the evaluation of programs offered in the school;

e. manage the school;

f. maintain order and discipline in the school and on the school grounds and at those other activities that are determined by the principal, with the teachers of the school, to be school activities;

g. promote co-operation between the school and the communities that it serves;

h. provide for the placement of students in courses of study and education programs prescribed or approved under this Act;

i. provide for the promotion and advancement of students;

j. evaluate or provide for the evaluation of teachers employed in the school;

k. annually provide a report with respect to the school;

l. ensure a student record is established and maintained for each student in the school;

m. where the school is a French first language school, promote cultural identity and French language in the school; and

n. carry out other duties assigned by the board.

Section 25(1) further adds that

A principal of a school shall establish a school council for the school.

As equally prescriptive, the *Prince Edward Island School Act* (1988) has this to say with respect to the duties of school principals:

The principal of a school shall, subject to the Minister's directives and the policies of the school board

a. be responsible for such school as may be assigned by the school board;

b. provide educational leadership in the school;

c. ensure that the instruction provided by teachers employed at the school is consistent with the courses of study and education programs prescribed, approved or authorized pursuant to this Act;

d. perform the supervisory, management and other duties required or assigned by the Unit Superintendent or the school board;

e. evaluate or make provision for the evaluation of teachers under the principal's supervision and report to the Unit Superintendent respecting the evaluation;

f. perform teaching duties as assigned by the school board;

g. maintain proper order and discipline in the school and on the school property and during activities sponsored or approved by the school board;

h. foster co-operation and co-ordination of effort among staff members of the school;

i. ensure records are maintained in respect of each student enrolled in the school in accordance with the regulations and school board policy;

j. ensure that teachers conduct such assessments as are appropriate to determine the progress and promotion of students as required by the Minister or the school board;

k. consult with teachers and promote such students as the principal considers proper and cause to be issued to students such statements, report cards or certificates as are appropriate;

l. report to the Unit Superintendent or to the school board as required on matters concerning the school;

m. attend to the health, comfort and safety of the students;

n. report notifiable, nuisance and regulated diseases to the Chief Health Officer;

o. encourage the establishment of and consult the School Council on matters relevant to its functions;

p. initiate the development of a school improvement plan.

Similarly, the *New Brunswick Education Act* (1997) states in Section 28 that

The principal of a school

a. is the educational leader and administrator of the school and has overall responsibility for the school and for the teachers and other school personnel employed at the school, and

b. is accountable to the superintendent of the school district for the performance of the principal's duties and the overall educational progress of the pupils enrolled in the school.

1. The duties of a principal include

a. preparing, in consultation with the Parent School Support Committee and the school personnel, a school improvement plan and co-ordinating its implementation,

b. preparing, for parents of the pupils enrolled in the school, an annual school performance report, and ensuring that that report is communicated to those parents and the school community,

b.1) submitting annually to the District Education Council concerned, through the superintendent of the school district, a copy of the school improvement plan and a copy of the annual school improvement report,

c. ensuring that reasonable steps are taken to create and maintain a safe and effective learning environment,

d. participating in the selection of school personnel for the school,

e. encouraging and facilitating the professional development of teachers and other school personnel employed at the school,

f. evaluating the performance of teachers and other school personnel employed at the school,

g. being accountable and responsible for funds provided to and raised for the school,

h. ensuring that provincial, school district and school policies are followed, and

i. ensuring the establishment of and participating in the operation of a Parent School Support Committee at the school.

Although the various schools/education acts across the country may vary slightly in the specific language used, three main themes are consistent throughout the legislation:

• instructional or educational leadership;

• maintenance of order and discipline; and

• accountability.

These themes are consistent with what the current literature on school leadership has to say (Fullan, 2001; Hoy & Miskel, 2001; Sergiovanni, 1995; Young & Levin, 2002). At first glance, to the neophyte school administrator, the never-ending list of duties and expectations articulated in the provincial legislation across Canada appears to be rather daunting. However, today's thinking on school leadership places considerable emphasis on collaborative and shared decision-making strategies (Fullan, 2001; Hoy & Miskel, 2001; Sergiovanni, 1995; Young & Levin, 2002) which in theory should assist and facilitate the school leader's everyday work of management and leadership. Not everyone in school leadership would agree with this assertion.

Conclusion

Other topics included in the various school/education acts range from the duties of school boards and school personnel, school councils, the financing of education, to the language of instruction. These provincial pieces of legislation are written in considerable detail and vary from approximately 42 pages in length (Prince Edward Island) to several hundred pages, 426 specifically, in the case of the province of Ontario. Added to these acts are sections entitled "Regulations," which as stated earlier, go into greater detail on the more specific aspects of the items covered in the acts.

These documents are not exactly user-friendly and are somewhat tedious and laborious to go over. However, this chapter has attempted, in layman's language, to give the reader a general overview as to what these education/school acts cover. For additional information the reader is referred to the web-site for the Canadian Legal Information Institute (www.canlii.org), a valuable resource providing the actual text of all provincial laws, including education.

For Discussion

1. As mentioned at the beginning of the chapter, K-12 education in Canada is a provincial responsibility. Discuss the advantages and disadvantages of this arrangement.

2. What would you see as the advantages and disadvantages if K-12 education in Canada were to become a federal responsibility?

3. According to provincial legislation, students in K-12 education have a statutory or legal duty to conduct themselves in a responsible manner while attending school. Discuss your perceptions of what this means for today's students.

4. The duties and responsibilities of a teacher are many, varied and rather complex

   a. Comment on the reality of these duties.

   b. Which would you consider to be the major or primary responsibilities? Explain.

5. The duties and responsibilities of a principal are also many, varied and rather complex.

   a. Are these realistic – explain.

   b. Given the multitude of duties/responsibilities, what do you think motivates a teacher to become a principal? Discuss.

   c. What might be some of the stressors that a principal might experience on a daily basis?

4

Teacher Collective Agreements

The majority of teachers working in primary, elementary and secondary schools in Canada work under a contract referred to as a collective agreement. Collective agreements are negotiated on behalf of teachers by their professional association (i.e., union). These negotiations may be conducted directly with the provincial government as is usually the case with "centralized" agreements; school boards are represented by their association which joins with government in the negotiating process. In the case of "decentralized" agreements the negotiations are between the school board/division and the teachers' professional association.

Among some of the areas covered in collective agreements are salary scales, hours of instruction, sick leave and other forms of leave, probationary and tenure contracts, disciplinary action, teacher evaluation, length of the school year, harassment and sexual harassment, grievance and arbitration procedures. These areas will vary from province to province.

There are examples of provinces which have a combination of both a centralized agreement and a decentralized agreement. In Nova Scotia the process utilized to arrive at an agreement is referred to as two-tier bargaining. There is one provincial agreement for all 9500 teachers which sets out wages, substitute teacher benefits, term contract benefits, long term disability, marking and preparation time, travel allowance and service awards among others. In addition to this provincial agreement, there are regional agreements with each of the 8 Nova Scotian school boards. These agreements deal with such areas as hiring practices, seniority provisions, leaves of absence, and special leave.

The provincial teachers' association and the government of each province and territory have their lists of demands and through a negotiation process, long and protracted, a tentative agreement extending over two or more years is eventually reached. The professional association then presents this tentative agreement to teachers to be voted on. If the agreement is accepted by a majority of teachers, it then becomes law and is in effect for the period of time negotiated.

This chapter examines collective agreements across Canada and highlights features of those agreements.

Centralized v. Decentralized Agreements

In a number of provinces (i.e., Newfoundland and Labrador; New Brunswick; Prince Edward Island; Saskatchewan) teachers operate under a centralized collective agreement meaning that one collective agreement covers all teachers working in primary, elementary and secondary schools. Several provinces operate under decentralized agreements meaning that there are a number of individualized teacher collective agreements in operation. These individualized agreements may be negotiated on a school district/division basis or by individual teacher associations. For example in the province of Alberta, there are 63 collective agreements currently in existence and these are between teachers in the various school districts in operation throughout the province and the local school board or district. Teachers in the province of Manitoba operate under 39 bargaining units with each bargaining unit representing teachers assigned to schools from K-12.

Specific Agreement Articles

This section will examine a number of specific articles found in teacher collective agreements throughout Canada.

Hours of Instruction

Most agreements will have a section or article specifying the actual hours of instruction per school day. For example the New Brunswick Teachers' Federation's collective agreement (September 1, 2000 – February 29, 2004) in Article 18.01 states the following:

- For the first three years of the Elementary School (including kindergarten) – minimum 4 hours, maximum 5.5 hours;
- For the remaining years of the Elementary School and the Middle School – minimum 5 hours, maximum 5.5 hours;
- For the High School years – minimum 5.5 hours, maximum 6 hours.

Closely connected to the hours of instruction per day is Article 19 of the New Brunswick Teachers' Collective Agreement which addresses the amount of teacher preparation time:

- Where local circumstances permit, teachers shall be allowed, within the hours of instruction during which teachers are required to teach and students are required to remain in class, a minimum of one preparation period of not less than thirty-five (35) minutes per day or an equivalent amount of preparation time based on a longer time period. It is understood that the Employer is not required to employ additional teachers in order to provide such preparation periods.

Several teacher collective agreements in Alberta are very specific in specifying the actual number of minutes teachers are required to teach. Article 13.2 of the Edmonton School District Number 7 Collective Agreement (2003-2006) is one such example:

- A teacher will not be assigned duties in excess of 1800 minutes per week, of which a maximum of 1430 minutes will be devoted to the instruction of pupils. A teacher may agree to be timetabled for instructional duties which may vary in the number of minutes assigned per week. A teacher shall not be assigned instructional duties which would exceed an average of 1430 minutes per week for any given school year. Assignable time will provide for instruction, supervision of students and professional activities such as inservice sessions, staff meetings, committee work and parent/teacher conferences.

Extracurricular Activities

One area of contention consistently cited in teacher collective agreements across Canada is that of extracurricular activities. Article 24 of the Nova Scotia Teachers' Union Provincial Agreement (January 1, 2002 – July 31, 2005) reads as follows:

While the parties consider it desirable that teachers participate in extracurricular activities, it is recognized by the parties bound by this Agreement that any involvement, such as participation, supervision, administration, direction, coaching by a teacher in extra-curricular activities shall be on a voluntary basis.

Similar in wording and intent is Article 29.02 of the Newfoundland and Labrador Teachers' Association Collective Agreement (September 1, 2001 – August 31, 2004):

It is agreed that extra-curricular activities are a desirable part of a well-rounded education.It is also agreed that the principal and staff of each school will determine the extra-curricular activities to be provided in their school. Notwithstanding this, a teacher's participation in any extra-curricular activity requires that teacher's consent.

Teacher Discipline

Another standard clause in teacher collective agreements is one dealing with teacher discipline. Article 28 of the Collective Agreement between the Winnipeg Teachers' Association and the Winnipeg School Division (July 1, 2003 – June 30, 2005) has this to say:

The imposition of discipline without just cause by the Division or any agent thereof in the form of written warning(s) and/or suspension(s) with or without pay shall be subject to the following provisions:

a. Where the Division or person(s) acting on behalf of the Division so disciplines any person covered by this Collective Agreement and where the affected person is not satisfied that the discipline is for just cause, the Division's action shall be deemed to be a difference between the parties to or persons bound by this Collective Agreement under Article 8 – Provisions for Settlement of Disputes During Currency of Agreement.

b. When such a difference is referred to a Board of Arbitration under Article 8, the Board of Arbitration shall have the power to:
uphold the discipline
rescind the discipline
vary or modify the discipline
order the board to pay all or part of any loss of pay and/or benefits in respect of the discipline
do one or more of the things set out in subclause (i), (ii), (iii), and (iv) above.

c. The written warning shall not include Performance Assessment and Development done pursuant to Policy GCN and/or any regulations and amendments thereto (hereinafter referred to as the policy), except where the implementation of said policy against a person covered by this Collective Agreement is for the purpose of disciplining said person.

d. The Association agrees that the Division has the right to suspend an employee with or without pay for just cause.

Titled "Disciplinary Action," Article 10 of the Newfoundland and Labrador Teachers' Association Collective Agreement (September 1, 2001 – August 31, 2004) is more specific and exhaustive:

10.01. Subject to Clause 12.01 (b), no teacher shall be suspended, dismissed, or otherwise disciplined except for just cause.

10.02. Any teacher who is suspended or dismissed shall be provided written notification within five (5) calendar days of any oral notification. Such written notification shall state the precise reason(s) for the suspension or dismissal and no reasons other than those stated in that notice may subsequently be advanced against the teacher in that particular disciplinary action.

10.03 (a). A copy of any document placed on a teacher's personal file, which might at any time be used against a teacher in any case of suspension, dismissal or disciplinary action, shall be supplied concurrently to the teacher. Before any such document is entered in the teacher's personal file, it shall be signed by the teacher for the sole purpose of certifying that it has been examined. If the teacher refuses to sign, the document shall be entered in the personal file with the notification that the teacher has refused to sign. A teacher shall be provided an opportunity to submit a written explanation as to why he/she refused to sign the document and the written explanation shall be entered into the teacher's personal file. Such explanation shall be provided by the teacher within ten (10) calendar days of receipt of the document. No occurrence or event, which is not documented in the teacher's personal file within ten (10) calendar days of the discovery and verification by the Employer, except a culminating occurrence or event, shall be used against the teacher in any case of suspension, dismissal or other disciplinary action.

Teacher Evaluation

Most collective agreements include a section articulating the various aspects of teacher evaluation. Teacher evaluation is generally spoken of in two forms: formative evaluation and summative evaluation. Article 14 of the Newfoundland and Labrador Teachers' Collective Agreement (September 1, 2001 to August 31, 2004) states the following:

14.01. The prime purpose of evaluation shall be the increased effectiveness of personnel in improving instruction and the educational environment.

14.02. (a). Subject to Clause 14.02(b), all evaluations, both formative and summative, shall be conducted openly and with the knowledge of the teacher(s) and the teacher(s) shall be informed as to which type of evaluation is being conducted

(b) For the purposes of this Article

i) formative evaluation is a process of evaluation which occurs to improve the professional performance of the teacher(s);

ii) summative evaluation is the process of evaluation which uses its results to make decisions in areas of employment;

iii) the evaluation of a probationary teacher shall be comprised of both formative and summative processes;

iv) any summative evaluation made on a tenured teacher must be preceded by a formative evaluation.

(c) The School Board shall consult with the teacher in determining the nature of the support which may be required to address suggestions for change and improvements.

(d) Probationary teachers will be given an opportunity to address concerns which may be identified during the evaluation process.

14.03 The results of such evaluation shall be made known to the teacher(s) concerned and where results of evaluations are produced in written form, a copy will be given to the teacher(s) concerned.

14.04 Proper security shall be maintained on teacher evaluation files. Documents related to a teacher's evaluation may be viewed only by the Director of Education, the assistant Director of Personnel, the Assistant Director of Programs, and/or the teacher's current school principal or vice-principal and the contents of the file shall be held in strictest confidence. Any other person wishing to view a teacher's file may do so only with the written consent of the teacher. Teachers shall be permitted to view their own files at any mutually convenient time during normal working office hours.

14.05 A School Board's teacher evaluation policy shall be consistent with the terms of the Collective Agreement. Teachers shall be consulted with regard to changes to existing teacher evaluation policy.

Less prescriptive but more philosophical is Article 45 (Evaluation of Teaching Staff) of the Nova Scotia Teachers' Union Collective Agreement (January 1, 2002 – July 31, 2005):

45.01 Each School Board shall have a functioning evaluation system.

45.02 Teacher evaluation policies shall be consistent with the following principles:

(i) The purpose of evaluation is to enhance learning through the provision of a formative process and a summative process.

(ii) The formative process shall be designed to improve teaching through the identification of ways to change teaching strategies, teaching environments or teaching behaviours.

(iii) The summative process shall be designed to supply information that will lead to the modification of assignments, such as placements in other positions, promotions or terminations.

(iv) The evaluation process shall be a co-operative and consultative one through which shared goals are articulated.

(v) The evaluation process shall respect the professional rights of teachers including the right:

(a) to reasonable job security;

(b) to a reasonable degree of professional discretion in the performance of their jobs;

(c) to reasonable participation in decisions concerning both professional and employment-related aspects of their jobs;

(d) to have decisions made on the basis of evidence;

(e) to be evaluated on relevant criteria;

(f) not to be evaluated on hearsay, rumour, or unsubstantiated complaints;

(g) to be evaluated according to comprehensible standards;

(h) to notice concerning when they will be evaluated;

(i) to know the results of their evaluation;

(j) to express a reaction to the results of their evaluation in a meaningful way;

(k) to a statement of the reasons for any action taken in their cases;

(l) to appeal adverse decisions and to have their views considered by a competent and unbiased authority;

(m) to orderly and timely evaluation;

(n) to humane evaluation procedures;

(o) to have their evaluation kept private and confidential;

(p) to evaluation procedures which are not needlessly intrusive into their professional activities;

(q) to have their private lives considered irrelevant to their evaluation;

(r) to have evaluation not be used coercively to obtain aims external to the legitimate purposes of evaluation;

(s) to nondiscriminatory criteria and procedures;

(t) not to have evaluation used to sanction the expression of unpopular views; and

(u) to an overall assessment of their performance that is frank, honest and consistent.

(vi) The evaluation shall respect the rights of the Employer subject to the provisions of any Professional Agreement between the Union and a School Board, including:

(a) to exercise supervision and to make personnel decisions intended to improve the quality of the education they provide;

(b) to collect information relevant to their supervisory and evaluative roles;

(c) to act on such relevant information in the best interest of the students; and

(d) to have the cooperation of the teaching staff in implementing and executing a fair and effective system of evaluation.

(The statements in this Article are from *Successful Teacher Evaluation*, Thomas McGreal, 1983, Alexandria, VA: Association for Supervision and Curriculum Development.)

Grievance and Arbitration

Underpinning any collective agreement are the important processes of grievance and arbitration. These are mediation strategies employed when there are disagreements in the interpretation and operationalization of various articles in a collective agreement. These strategies facilitate settlements of issues without stoppages of work.

Teacher collective agreements usually contain clauses outlining the various steps to be followed; however, should this not be the case, reference is made to the province's other existing labor laws which have appropriate articles dedicated to these conflict resolution strategies.

The Grievance Process

Generally, grievance is the first step in resolving conflict between teachers and their employer. Collective agreements usually contain very specific Timelines outlining when and to whom complaints have to be made. The approach is an incremental one beginning with, in most cases, the on-site or building supervisor (i.e., the principal) meeting with the aggrieved (i.e., the teacher). Both parties to the complaint are represented: the teacher by a designate of the teachers' association and the on-site supervisor (principal) by the employer (i.e., the school board). Should this meeting fail to resolve the issue, the next step in the process is to meet with someone higher up in the "chain of command" – usually, the superintendent/director of the school board or a designate. After meeting with a school board designate and should this prove to be unsuccessful, the next step would be to meet with a designate of the ministry/department of education (usually the deputy minister or assistant deputy minister). If a resolution to the grievance continues to be unattainable, the minister of the ministry/department of education can refer the matter to an arbitration hearing.

Article 42 of the Nova Scotia Teachers' Union Collective Agreement (2002 – 2005) speaks at length to the grievance process:

42.01 The parties agree that a grievance means a dispute or difference of opinion concerning the interpretation or an alleged violation of any provision of this Agreement.

42.02 The following may lodge a grievance:

(a) a teacher on the teacher's own behalf or on behalf of the teacher and one (1) or more other teachers. In the latter case the other teachers shall affix their signatures to the written grievance;

(b) the Union;

(c) the Employer or the Minister's designate.

42.03 Grievances shall be processed in the manner hereinafter set forth:

(a) (i) Teachers' Informal Discussions

Within thirty (30) clear days of the effective knowledge of the facts which give rise to an alleged grievance, the teacher(s) shall discuss the matter with the Regional Education Officer. The Officer shall answer the matter within ten (10) days of the discussions. When any matter cannot be settled by the foregoing internal procedure, it shall be deemed to be a "grievance" and the following procedure shall apply provided said teacher(s) has/have the approval of the Union in writing or is represented by the Union.

(ii) Union's Informal Discussions

Where the Union is the grievor, the Union shall, within thirty (30) clear days of the effective knowledge of the facts which gives rise to an alleged grievance, meet with the Regional Education Officer to discuss the matter. The Regional Education Officer shall answer the matter within ten (10) days of the discussions. Where any matter cannot be settled by the foregoing informal procedure, it shall be deemed to be a "grievance" and the procedure in Step One, Step Two and Step Three shall be followed.

(iii) For purposes of 42.03 (a) (ii), in the case of hirings subsequent to the signing of this agreement, "effective knowledge" regarding the contract status of teachers shall occur on receipt of the lists pursuant to Article 48.01 and Article 48.02 or on receipt of specific information pursuant to Article 48.03 provided the effective date of the contract and "effective knowledge" fall within the same school year for which the lists were generated.

Grievance

Step One – The aggrieved party shall, within ten (10) clear days of the receipt of the reply pursuant to (a) present the grievance in writing to one of the Executive Directors of Education (or designate), who shall arrange to meet with the aggrieved party and/or the aggrieved party's representative within the next ten (10) clear days and at a time which is agreeable to both the aggrieved party and the executive Director (or designate).

Within five (5) clear days of said meeting, the Executive Director (or designate) shall forward the written decision to the aggrieved party and the Union. If the written decision reached after Step One is acceptable to the Union, then the decision shall be final and binding on the Minister of Education, the Union and the teachers and if applicable, the School Board(s).

Step Two – If the decision in Step One is not acceptable, the Union may within twenty (20) clear days present the grievance to the Deputy Minister of Education (or designate) and the Deputy Minister shall arrange to meet with the Union within ten (10) clear days at a time which is agreeable to both parties. Within five (5) clear days the Deputy Minister shall forward the written decision to the Union. If the written decision reached after Step Two is acceptable to the Union, then the decision shall be final and binding on the Minister of Education, the Union and the teachers and if applicable, the School Board(s).

Step Three – If the decision in Step Two is not acceptable, the Union may within twenty (20) clear days refer the matter to an arbitrator. The arbitrator shall be chosen by mutual agreement between the parties. If within five (5) clear days the parties are unable to agree upon an arbitrator, the appointment shall be made by the Minister of Environment and Labour, upon the request of either party.

(b) The Employer or Designate

Step One – The aggrieved party shall within thirty (30) clear days of the effective knowledge of the facts which give rise to an alleged grievance present the grievance in writing to the Executive Director of the Union, who shall arrange to meet with the aggrieved party and/or its representative within the next ten (10) days, and at a time which is agreeable to both the aggrieved party and the Executive Director of the Union. Within five (5) clear days of said meeting, the Executive Director (or designate) shall forward the written decision to the aggrieved party.

Step Two – If the decision in Step One is not acceptable the aggrieved party may within twenty (20) clear days present the grievance in writing to the President of the Union (or designate), who shall arrange to meet with the aggrieved party and/or its representative within the next ten (10) clear days, and at a time which is agreeable to both the aggrieved party and the President of the Union (or designate). Within five (5) clear days of said meeting the President of the Union (or designate) shall forward the written decision to the aggrieved party.

Step Three – If the decision in Step Two is not acceptable, the Minister may within twenty (20) clear days refer the matter to an arbitrator. The arbitrator shall be chosen by mutual agreement between the parties. If within five (5) clear days the parties are unable to agree upon an arbitrator, the appointment shall be made by the Minister of Environment and Labour, upon the request of either party.

42.04 The arbitrator shall, after considering the grievance, render the decision within fourteen (14) clear days and forthwith send a written copy of the decision to both parties.

42.05 The decision of the arbitrator shall not alter, amend, or modify any provisions of the Professional Agreement.

42.06 The decision of the arbitrator shall be final and binding on the Minister of Education, the Union and the teachers, and if applicable, the School Boards.

42.07 If advantage of the provisions of this Article has not been taken within the time limits stipulated herein, the grievance shall be deemed to have been abandoned. On the other hand, the grievor(s) may proceed to the next step in the case of absence of a stipulated meeting or answer within the stipulated time limits. Said time limits may be extended by mutual written agreement.

42.08 (i) Notwithstanding the procedures outlined in 42.03, any decision acceptable to an aggrieved party at any stage of the grievance procedure shall commence to be implemented within thirty (30) clear days after having been rendered, unless the parties agree to a later implementation date.

(ii) Should the implementation progress be unsatisfactory to the Union, the Union may refer the matter directly to an arbitrator.

Conclusion

This chapter has given an overview of teacher collective agreements across Canada. Although differing somewhat from province to province, the overall intent from the perspectives of teachers' professional associations is to provide optimal working conditions for their teachers in the nation's classrooms. From the other side of the bargaining table, it would appear that provincial governments and the various school districts seem to be more intent on saving money. Creating the best teaching and learning conditions for our K-12 students across the country does not always appear to be the primary motivation when parties sit down at the negotiating table. Unfortunately, the politics of education is alive and well and tends to characterize and often impede what should always be the primary goal of teachers' collective bargaining alluded to above – that of creating the best teaching and learning conditions for our students.

On a more pragmatic level, teachers and school administrators are encouraged to be knowledgeable of the specific articles in their agreements and when individual articles are less than clear and understandable, they should seek clarification and explanation from their professional associations.

For Discussion

1. Are teachers and school administrators generally familiar with their collective agreements? Why or why not?

2. The process of collective bargaining usually leads to a collective agreement. From your observations as an educator, what can you say, positive or negative, about this process?

3. Comment on a couple of priority items you have observed in recent collective bargaining sessions. Why would you consider these to be priority items?

4. Are there items usually not included in teachers' collective agreements that you think should be included? Elaborate.

5

Due Process

Conflict is an inevitable aspect of the everyday work of teachers and school administrators. In that everyday conflict it is important that teachers and administrators exercise due process in their dealings and relationships with colleagues and students. In matters of a legal nature it becomes even more important that due process is exercised. According to Keel (1998), "the concept of due process is often used interchangeably with terms such as fair process, fairness, natural justice, and fundamental justice; in other words, the requirement of acting fairly in exercising any authority over other persons" (p. 127). MacKay (1984) has added further clarification as to what due process is all about:

> Natural justice is a basic concept rooted in common law, the Magna Carta, and the Bible. The term has a technical legal meaning and is not, as one might think, a simple meting-out of justice. The heart of natural justice is fair procedures; it is analogous to the U.S. concept of "due process." There are two premises of natural justice: first, a decision-maker should not be biased; second, an opportunity to be heard should be given to those affected by a decision. (p. 31)

Student Matters

Due process becomes an issue when teachers experience discipline problems with students. One of the most common criticisms of teachers by students is that "the teacher wasn't fair." This criticism speaks directly to this notion of due process or procedural fairness. As mentioned in Chapter 2, it is important that students be treated with dignity and respect which hopefully results in a considerable degree of fairness.

Consider the example of a teacher experiencing many difficulties teaching a group of Grade 8 students. Losing his patience because students refuse to pay attention, the teacher informs students that they all have a recess period detention with him after this particular class. In all probability not every student is responsible for the mayhem in the class and the legitimate question that arises is whether or not it is fair to detain all students during recess period.

Teachers sometimes make such a decision out of frustration and with very little forethought. There may be considerable fallout from this decision resulting in irate telephone calls from parents to the principal's office. The principal is then called upon to do some damage control.

In hindsight, the teacher in question should not have backed himself in the corner and taken a course of action which instead of solving the problem, further exacerbates an already difficult situation. Upon reflection, the teacher would have been better served by dealing with those particular students who have initiated the disruption on a one-on-one basis.

Students will accept discipline, albeit somewhat reluctantly, from teachers and school administrators as long as they perceive that they are being treated in a fair and reasonable manner. Parents, being the chief advocates for their sons and daughters, will do likewise.

In matters dealing with out-of-school suspensions, it is incumbent upon the school administration to comply with the various protocols put in place by school board policy which is in line with the provincial education or schools act.

Teacher Matters

There are times when conflict happens between teachers. All provincial teacher associations have codes of ethics which stipulate how such matters should be handled. Essentially, the first step is for teachers to talk to each other and express their specific concerns. If this does not solve the problem, teachers may involve the school administration and a process of mediation is followed which hopefully results in a satisfactory solution to the parties involved.

Should this not be the case, the teachers may go the next step and involve their professional association which has established procedures in place to deal with such situations. The emphasis in all these dealings is on giving both parties an opportunity to be heard. When provincial associations get involved, the ideal is to come to a resolution of the problem which is acceptable to both parties. If such is not the case, the association will usually impose a solution that both parties are expected to live with.

Generally speaking, the preferred solution is one that can be negotiated in house meaning at the teacher to teacher level. Having to involve the school administration causes additional stress and anxiety for those teachers. However, it is not always possible for teachers to resolve these conflictual situations by themselves and it may be necessary to request the assistance of the school administration. School administrators usually have more experience in these matters and they may be able to assist the teachers in working out a compromise.

Legal Matters

Teachers and administrators could find themselves involved in a legal situation involving a court of law or a quasi-legal tribunal. According to Dickinson and MacKay (1989), "one must attempt to maintain an even hand in affording people rights and ensuring that a decision-making process does not become overladen with red tape" (p. 636).

MacKay (cited in Dickinson & MacKay, 1989) offers this caveat on the importance of fairness and natural justice in these procedures:

> One of the important roles played by the courts is to ensure that proper decision-making procedures are followed. This is particularly true in matters of employment where a decision may affect a person's livelihood. However, the courts must be careful not to hamper decision-makers by imposing too many procedural rules. Indeed, one person's due process may well be another person's red tape. [In a case in Nova Scotia] . . . the board of appeal hearing lasted for sixteen days, yet one of the grounds for review was that the teacher had not been given an adequate hearing before the original school board.
>
> The question is what, in light of many factors, is the simplest and most expeditious way of ensuring a reasonable opportunity to a party to know and respond to prejudicial data. Among these factors is the interest of the tribunal in getting on with its job. It would be unrealistic and wrong, in my opinion, to hamstring a tribunal with formal hearing procedures if substantial justice or procedural fairness can be achieved by informal means. (p. 636)

Conclusion

Due process is often referred to as natural justice, or procedural fairness. Whatever the term used, it is important for teachers and administrators to demonstrate such fairness in all dealings with students and colleagues. The perhaps over-used cliché, "it is not only good that justice be done but that it be perceived to be done" is one that should be kept in mind at all times. Although we tend to think of due process as a legal term, most teachers and administrators will not experience this term in a courtroom setting. Rather, it is one which will characterize our relationships and interactions in the classroom and in our faculty lounges. Attempting to practise due process as practically as possible in these settings should result in interactions of a positive nature for all concerned.

For Discussion

1. What is the perception of teachers in general regarding the concept of due process? Elaborate.

2. Are students aware of due process? Explain.

3. Teachers and school administrators are often referred to as "moral exemplars." Discuss this concept in terms of due process.

6

Teacher Liability and Negligence

Teacher liability and negligence are subjects that can cause teachers and administrators considerable anxiety and a significant degree of paranoia. This chapter examines these topics and puts forth some practical advice in order to minimize, as is reasonably possible, those fears and anxieties.

Liability Defined

Simply stated, liability refers to "responsibility for one's conduct" (Yogis, 1995, p. 131). Considering the wide range of duties teachers are responsible for in the everyday work of teaching, this definition is an all-encompassing one which teachers need to take very seriously.

On the surface, teacher liability is a neutral term denoting responsibility. The problem arises when teachers are guilty of negligence and end up in the principal's or district superintendent's office or provincial courtroom attempting to defend their behaviors involving students they have taught or supervised.

Negligence

Negligence refers to ." . . the omitting to do something that a reasonable [person] would do or the doing of something that a reasonable [person] would not do" (adapted from the *Canadian Law Dictionary's* definition of negligence, p. 153). Note the two inherent concepts in this definition: the act of omission and the act of commission. Teachers and administrators make hundreds, perhaps thousands of decisions in the course of a regular school day and it is not unrealistic to assume that a percentage of those decisions would be imprudent decisions resulting in negligence or alleged negligence.

Four Step Analysis

MacKay and Sutherland (1992) have referred to a four step analysis which is useful in determining whether or not there has been negligence on the part of the teacher or administrator. These steps are as follows:

1. Was a duty of care owed to the injured person?

2. What is the standard of care required by the situation?

3. Was this standard of care breached?

4. What damages, if any, were suffered by the injured person? (p. 1)

Duty of care refers to teachers having a responsibility to provide reasonable care and supervision to students placed in their charge. Step number 1 simply asks whether or not there was a responsibility on the part of the teacher to provide that reasonable care and supervision. Brown and Zuker (2002) point out that "where there is no statutory or common law duty to ensure the safety or wellbeing of another person, there cannot be a finding of liability in negligence if the person is injured" (p. 80). Because educators are acting *in loco parentis* they have an obligation by law to care for students in a safe and prudent manner, comparable to the care that parents would be expected to provide.

Standard of care stems from duty of care and is more specific. What is the actual standard or level of care expected of the teacher when supervising this particular student or group of students? The underlying issue in determining this standard of care is to identify "whether a reasonable and prudent degree of care has been exercised" (Dougherty, 2004, p. 16). For example: one would suggest that a primary teacher supervising Grade 1 students on the playground would be expected to be much more vigilant than if it were students at the intermediate or junior high level playing on the playground. The age of the student and the activity the student is engaged in are significant factors to be taken into consideration.

Generally speaking, the teacher is not expected to eliminate any or all possibility of harm or injury. However, there is an expectation that every reasonable precaution be taken to reduce any potential danger that is "reasonably foreseeable" (MacKay & Flood, 2001, p. 376).

Brown and Zuker (2002) state that the application of the standard of care

. . . will depend upon the number of students being supervised at any given time, the nature of the exercise or activity in progress, the age and the degree of skill and training which the students may have received in connection with such activity, the nature and condition of the equipment in use at the time, the competency and capacity of the students involved, and a host of other matters which may be widely varied but which, in a given case, may affect the application of the prudent-parent standard to the conduct of the school authority in the circumstances. (p. 86)

With respect to breaching the standard of care, did the teacher act appropriately and professionally in the execution of his/her supervisory responsibilities? If the answer to that question is an affirmative one, then there is no negligence on the part of the teacher. If the teacher has not acted appropriately and professionally, then the analysis proceeds to the number four step.

This final step involves a determination of whether or not there have been any damages or injury to the person in question. There can be no negligence if there are no damages or injury.

Bezeau (1995) has emphasized the concept of "causal proximity" when discussing negligence. He goes on to state that causal proximity requires that the damage suffered by the victim must be the result of negligent action or inaction. Bezeau further noted that negligent behavior is not necessarily the only cause of damage; often times damage is not caused directly by the negligent behavior but by an event that is the result of negligent behavior.

There should be an obvious connection between the resulting injury and the actions or failure to act by the teacher (Shariff, 2004). Shariff goes on to state that "a factual link between the supervisor's breach of the standard of care and the plaintiff's injuries" (p. 142) must be established in order for the court to deem a teacher negligent.

Kitchen and Corbett (1995) have referred to a technique known as the "but-for-test" (p. 22) commonly used by courts to determine the cause of an injury. This is accomplished through answering the simple question of whether or not the injury would have happened if it were not for the actions of the defendant. In cases where this point cannot be proven and the immediate cause of the injury is the result of some extenuating factor unrelated to the defendant's behavior or lack of behavior, then the defendant cannot be at fault.

Contributory Negligence

In Canada courts consider the principle of contributory negligence when settling negligence or liability suits. Contributory negligence involves dividing the responsibilities of the negligent act between the accused and the victim. In certain cases the teacher is not the sole individual responsible for injuries or damages incurred as a result of negligence. Depending on the age of the student and the circumstances surrounding the specific incident, the student can be found to have contributed directly to the injury or damage. Students do have a duty or obligation to act with reasonable care for their own safety (Brown & Zuker, 2002). This would obviously involve students of an older age, specifically at the junior or senior high levels.

An example of a court decision involving contributory negligence is Kowalchuk v. Middlesex County Board of Education (Anderson, 1992, pp. 33 – 34). This case involved a student being injured as a result of jumping on a gym mat left outside the gymnasium door. The school board was found to be 80 percent negligent and the student 20 percent contributorily negligent. In essence, the court had determined that the student was 20 percent responsible for his own injury.

Vicarious Liability

According to the Canadian Law Dictionary (Yogis, 1995), vicarious liability is defined as follows:

> the imputed responsibility of one person for the acts of another; occurs "when the law holds one person responsible for the misconduct of another, although he is himself free from blameworthiness or fault. It is therefore an instance of strict (no fault) liability. (p. 237)

In the context of education, vicarious liability refers to holding a school board responsible for the negligent acts of an employee committed during the course of that employee's work on behalf of the school board.

This form of liability was established in part to help teachers and administrators found guilty of negligence to avoid all or part of the monetary damages awarded to plaintiffs. Even when not blamed directly for the incident in question, the school board in most cases assumes liability for the incident and either pays the damages itself or has them covered by its insurance company. School boards carry liability coverage for such purposes. School boards do have the right to initiate legal proceedings against employees found guilty in negligence cases in order to recover monies awarded victims. However, as indicated by Brown (1998), ". . . this is rarely done" (p. 106).

In a recent case Justice Faour of the Newfoundland and Labrador Supreme Court Trial Division found the Avalon East School Board vicariously liable for the sexual assault of a student by one of its teachers (John Doe v. Avalon East School Board, 2004). His reasons were as follows:

1. John Doe was subject to the Board's authority on that day, and such authority was exercised by Neary, the board's employee.

2. The assault took place on the school property, during school hours, during the time Doe was in class, and at the time, Neary was responsible for providing instruction to Doe in the computer class in which he was enrolled.

3. As a teacher, Neary had a significant degree of professional and legislated authority over his students. He was in a position of trust vis a vis his students.

4. It was the direct abuse of that trust, and the authority granted by the School Board, which was involved in Neary's assault upon Doe. (Callahan, 2004. n. p.)

Implications for Teachers and Administrators

Given the foregoing commentary it is little wonder that teachers and administrators can become stressed out and paranoid about these issues of liability and negligence. However, teachers and administrators who conduct their everyday work as educators with a reasonable modicum of caution and common sense, will in all probability never have to deal with being charged with negligence and having to face a judge in that most intimidating of all human institutions, the court.

The Classroom

The classroom being the locale where most teachers and students spend a significant percentage of their time, it is important for teachers to ensure that there are no physical challenges to student safety present in that classroom. An example of this could be a student desk that has a part broken which has resulted in a very sharp edge capable of cutting a student. Any damaged item in the classroom should be removed immediately and passed along to maintenance personnel for repair. Students in classrooms should be supervised to the degree that supervision is warranted and as mentioned previously, the age of students is a significant factor to be taken into consideration.

Physical Education, Science, Industrial Arts and Home Economics Areas

The gymnasium, science, industrial arts and home economics areas are ones where teachers have to be particularly vigilant of situations that could present challenges liability-wise. Again, common sense and a reasonable degree of caution are highly advised. Periodic spot checks of equipment and the facilities themselves are recommended. It is suggested that these spot checks be built into the teacher's regular routine – perhaps at the beginning of each week, thus establishing a pattern not easily forgotten.

Administrators

The principal is ultimately responsible for everything that happens in the school building and consequently the onus is on the principal to ensure that nothing is left to chance with respect to negligence and liability. The areas of concern here can be divided into two categories: physical and pedagogical. By physical is meant the actual school building and anything in or around the building that can constitute a physical threat to the safety of its patrons. Specific areas administrators should pay close attention to are: sidewalks and parking lots, especially in the winter months (i.e., ice and snow build-up), doors (especially the levers referred to as panic hardware), stairwells, and ceilings.

It is recommended that administrators do a complete walkabout of the school property which would include outside and all rooms inside the building at least a couple of times per week. Ideally and as mentioned previously, this type of inspection should be built into the routine schedule of the administrator and any concerns should be brought to the attention of the maintenance person in the school or the district maintenance department. It is further recommended that a record be kept of such inspections and any requests for follow-up maintenance.

With respect to the pedagogical area, this refers to teachers doing the work they were hired to do – teaching and covering the required curriculum. Commonly referred to as teacher evaluation by teachers, professional development is the euphemism adopted by district office personnel. This is a fairly detailed process set out by school districts for principals to follow to ensure that teachers are acting in accord with their professional responsibilities. The clinical supervision model is widely used by districts and consists of a number of conferences with the principal as well as in-class observations of teachers teaching their lessons. Ideally, these sessions should lead to principals identifying any concerns of a pedagogical nature. Principals are then expected to work with teachers to remediate those concerns.

This aspect of the principal's work is included in this section on negligence and liability because should a principal fail to fulfill this expectation of his position and something negative happen to a student as a result of unprofessional teacher behavior, a case could be made legally that the principal should have been aware of such potential negative teacher behavior and should have taken preventative action. Realistically speaking, it is practically impossible for the principal to be aware of all such potential negative behaviors but that does not prevent a parent or lawyer from pursuing that line of argument. No one expects the school principal to be aware of everything negative that is or might be happening in the school building; however, it is expected that the principal take reasonable and common-sensical measures to prevent negative happenings, be they physical or pedagogical, from occurring.

Conclusion

This chapter has examined the various intricacies of teacher liability and negligence. It is important to keep in mind that no amount of safeguarding will completely eliminate the various hazards that students will come into contact with in the school system. Teachers and school administrators are human beings complete with their imperfections and highly capable of making mistakes. However, this section has attempted to provide teachers and administrators with some sage and practical advice which should be helpful in assisting them to avoid accusations of liability and negligence.

Caution and common sense are the operative words when involved in working with students in schools. Schools are animated places where students are engaged in all sorts of learning activities and teachers and administrators are right in the thick of all that activity. Suffice it to say that as long as teachers and school administrators exercise that caution and common sense, the reality is that students will experience a positive school experience, devoid hopefully, of the negatives alluded to above.

For Discussion

1. Should educators be concerned about liability and negligence? Discuss.

2. List a number of strategies teachers in the following classroom situations could utilize to minimize the development of negligent situations:

a) Regular classroom

b) Chemistry lab

c) Gymnasium

d) Industrial Arts "shop"

e) Art room.

3. What are the current attitudes of students and parents towards teacher negligence? Elaborate.

4. With all this talk about teacher liability and negligence there is a very real danger that both teachers and school administrators will develop a certain degree of paranoia. What advice would you share with these two groups to help minimize that paranoia?

7

Corporal Punishment

The term, corporal punishment, conjures up images in days gone by of teachers strapping students for the most trivial of reasons such as not knowing how to spell a word or for not knowing the answer to a question from their Social Studies textbook. This chapter discusses what is meant by corporal punishment and examines the relevant provincial and federal legislation. Practical advice is given on alternative measures to corporal punishment and how teachers can create a positive classroom climate designed to do what corporal punishment attempted to do, albeit unsuccessfully, in the past.

Corporal Punishment Defined

LaMorte (1999) defines corporal punishment as "the use of such physical contact as striking, paddling, or spanking of a student by an educator" (p. 129). He adds that

> Although once widely used, it is a controversial practice that has received much debate. Proponents view it as a necessary and educationally sound disciplinary measure. Those opposed view the practice as archaic, cruel, and inhuman and an unjustifiable act on the part of the state. (p. 129)

Brown and Zuker (2002) refer to corporal punishment as "a disciplinary measure which involves intentionally creating discomfort or pain in the student by physical means" (p. 132).

Another definition proffered by Strauss and Donnelly (1993) states that corporal punishment is "the use of physical force with the intention of causing a child to experience pain but not injury, for purposes of correction or control of the child's behaviour" (p. 419). They further add the following behaviors to that definition:

> (1) spanking or slapping administered to the hand, clothed buttocks, or leg; (2) grabbing or shoving with more force than is needed; (3) shaking or pulling hair; (4) hitting or slapping of the head, face, or bare buttocks; and/or (5) hitting with belts, paddles, hair brushes, sticks and other objects. (p. 420)

Although these various definitions suggest that pain is necessary to induce compliance, the research on corporal punishment "paints a dismal picture" (Brown & Zuker, 2002, p. 192). Many studies have concluded that the use of corporal punishment is ineffective, offensive, and may result in harmful psychological effects which may last well into adulthood (Imbrogno, 2000).

Provincial and Federal Legislation

Educationally and from a psychological perspective, corporal punishment does not make any sense but legally, the practice is allowed in some Canadian jurisdictions and under certain conditions is condoned federally. According to MacKay and Sutherland (2006), "the education acts of Alberta, Saskatchewan, Manitoba, and Ontario still allow corporal punishment" (p. 24). However, they do point out that many school districts in those provinces have initiated district-wide bans on the use of corporal punishment.

Section 43 of the Criminal Code of Canada condones the use of corporal punishment:

> Every schoolteacher, parent or person standing in the place of a parent is justified in using force by way of correction toward a pupil or child, as the case may be, who is under his care, if the force does not exceed what is reasonable under the circumstances. (http://www.canlii.org/ca/sta/c-46/sec43.html)

Over the years there have been considerable controversy and debate over this section of the Criminal Code and a number of legal challenges have been launched all the way to the Supreme Court of Canada. These challenges have been on behalf of several civil liberties groups and have argued that this section violated various rights outlined in the *Canadian Charter of Rights and Freedoms*.

The latest challenge to Section 43 came from the Canadian Foundation for Children, Youth and the Law in 2003. The Supreme Court of Canada heard arguments from this Foundation that Section 43 violated the constitutional rights of children, specifically legal rights (sections 7 and 12) and equality rights (section 15) as outlined in the *Canadian Charter of Rights and Freedoms*.

In early 2004 the Supreme Court of Canada, by a margin of 6-3, handed down their decision upholding the constitutionality of Section 43. Chief Justice Beverley McLachlin stated that the general rule is that parents and teachers should avoid criminal prosecution if they use "only minor corrective force of a transitory and trifling nature." The following criteria for using corporal punishment were also put forth in the Supreme Court's decision:

1. corporal punishment of children under two years of age and teenagers is banned;

2. parents cannot use any objects while disciplining their children;

3. punishment must be administered with an open hand;

4. blows or slaps to the head are prohibited;

5. the force cannot cause harm, be degrading or cruel, or administered out of anger; and

6. the gravity of a child's precipitating behaviour is irrelevant.

(http://www.canlii.org/ca/cas/scc/2004/2004scc4.html)

In addition to the above criteria for parents, the Court issued more restrictive guidelines for teachers allowing them to use force only in situations to restrain students – such as when breaking up a fight. It is imperative that teachers be aware of this development as it points out quite definitively that they cannot use physical force in the classroom in a routine manner as has been the custom in the past. A student is behaving in an obnoxious manner or uses vulgarity towards a teacher; the teacher responds by hitting the student. Under this new criterion stated above, Section 43 can no longer be used as a defence for such teacher behavior. The best advice for teachers is that under no circumstances should they engage in physical force when dealing with students no matter what the offensive behavior is. The only exception of course would be in the case of their attempting to break up a fight between students or where another individual is in imminent danger of being injured by the student in question.

Alternatives to Corporal Punishment

Teaching is a challenging occupation. Classrooms consisting of 25 – 35 students, all with their individual personalities, are quite common in Canadian schools. No wonder there will be times when the patience of the teacher is tested and there are occasions that have the potential to result in the use of physical force. Classroom management is indeed the major challenge confronted by teachers in their everyday work with students. The importance of effective classroom management is underscored by Levin, Nolan, Kerr and Elliot (2004): "the most thoroughly prepared and well-designed lesson has no chance of success if the instructor is not able to effectively manage the classroom and her students' behavior. Extreme cases of poor management, in fact, lead to poor learning" (pp. 1-2). Libraries have been written on classroom management and the one obvious commonality of all of these writings is that corporal punishment is not an effective classroom management strategy to use in the classroom.

Years ago corporal punishment was used routinely to deal with disruptive and non-co-operative students. Times have changed the way we look at classroom management and corporal punishment. Nowadays the emphasis when dealing with chronic behavioral problems is on teachers building positive relationships with students and breaking the cycle of discouragement (Levin et al., 2004). The author has always maintained that there is something drastically wrong if we as teachers have to physically beat students to get them to learn; the teaching-learning process is all about relating to and connecting with students. For a more in-depth discussion on a variety of strategies to use in the classroom, the reader is referred to a publication by Levin et al. (2004) listed in the References section of this book.

Conclusion

This chapter has taken a brief look at corporal punishment and the relevant provincial and federal legislation. Although not statutorily banned in all Canadian provinces, this practice is, for all intents and purposes, totally unacceptable in our schools. Teachers and school administrators need to use positive classroom management practices which have as their goal the motivation of students in order to succeed in the teaching-learning process. The use of corporal punishment in the past only exacerbated an already difficult and negative relationship between the student and the teacher/school administrator. No strategy can take the place of a mutual respect between student and the teacher/school administrator, and that can only be initiated and fostered with a variety of the positive strategies alluded to above.

For Discussion

1. How have society's attitudes towards corporal punishment changed over the years? Elaborate.

2. As a parent, why might you object to the use of corporal punishment in schools?

3. Suggest a variety of discipline strategies that could be effectively used in the classroom.

4. What values should underpin any discipline strategies utilized in the classroom? Elaborate.

8

Sexual Assault

In recent years there has been a preponderance of sexual assault activity perpetuated by a variety of individuals in supervisory relationships over children. One of the groups often mentioned in the media is that of teachers. Male teachers feel particularly vulnerable especially if they work in elementary schools where it is not all that uncommon for younger students to get "touchy, feely" (i.e., huggy bear-ish, so to speak) with their teachers.

This chapter will examine the legislation on sexual assault and its implications for the conduct of teachers. Practical suggestions will be offered as to how teachers should behave both in and outside the classroom to ensure that they act in a highly professional manner at all times.

Criminal Code of Canada

It is an offence under the *Criminal Code of Canada* to touch directly or indirectly, any part of a body of a young person for a sexual purpose; such behavior is punishable by imprisonment up to a maximum period of 10 years. Teachers should be aware of the following sections of the Criminal Code:

151. Every person who, for a sexual purpose, touches, directly or indirectly, with a part of the body or with an object, any part of the body of a person under the age of fourteen years,

(a) is guilty of an indictable offence and liable to imprisonment for a term not exceeding ten years and to a minimum punishment of imprisonment for a term of forty-five days; or

(b) is guilty of an offence punishable on summary conviction and liable to imprisonment for a term not exceeding eighteen months and to a minimum punishment of imprisonment for a term of fourteen days.

152. Every person who, for a sexual purpose, invites, counsels or incites a person under the age of fourteen years to touch, directly or indirectly, with a part of the body or with an object, the body of any person, including the body of the person who so invites, counsels or incites and the body of the person under the age of fourteen years,

(a) is guilty of an indictable offence and liable to imprisonment for a term not exceeding ten years and to a minimum punishment of imprisonment for a term of forty-five days; or

(b) is guilty of an offence punishable on summary conviction and liable to imprisonment for a term not exceeding eighteen months and to a minimum punishment of imprisonment for a term of fourteen days.

153. (1) Every person commits an offence who is in a position of trust or authority towards a young person, who is a person with whom the young person is in a relationship of dependency or who is in a relationship with a young person that is exploitative of the young person, and who

(a) for a sexual purpose, touches, directly or indirectly, with a part of the body or with an object, any part of the body of the young person; or

(b) for a sexual purpose, invites, counsels or incites a young person to touch, directly or indirectly, with a part of the body or with an object, the body of any person, including the body of the person who so invites, counsels or incites and the body of the young person.

(http://www.canlii.org/ca/sta/c-46/sec153.1.html)

There have been cases of sexual assault against teachers which have turned out to be false. Consider this example cited by MacKay and Sutherland, (2006):

In R. v. C. B. a teacher was charged with sexual assault when a student alleged that the teacher had touched her left shoulder, then moved his hand to her left breast. The judge observed that it would be unusual for this teacher to put his hand on the student's chair or shoulder when offering assistance in class. He held that the act of touching a student's shoulder was not prudent in today's school setting. He found that the touching of a student's breast would be imprudent and subject to criminal charges. In this case, the teacher was acquitted, primarily because the trial judge preferred the teacher's evidence over the student's when he denied ever touching her breast. The relative credibility of the victim and the accused is often at the heart of such cases where there is no other corroborating evidence. (p. 30)

Teachers and school administrators are very vulnerable to the accusations of students. It is imperative that they be very cautious in their behaviors towards children. Avoiding any unnecessary contact is wise advice especially at the higher levels of schooling (i.e., upper elementary, junior and senior high). At the primary and lower elementary levels students very commonly hug their teachers; it is not suggested that teachers reject overt signs of affection. However, teachers should act professionally and with moderation in these situations. Teachers need to be conservative in the degree of affection they show their students, depending of course on the particular situation they find themselves in.

Practical Advice

In a paper presented at the Canadian Association for the Practical Study of Law (CAPSLE) 1999 annual conference, lawyer Eleanor Doctor put forth the following common sense tips for avoiding false allegations of sexual misconduct:

• Know your students and development psychology well.

• Avoid closing your classroom door particularly when you are with a single student.

• Place your desk so that your activity behind the desk can be easily observed from the classroom entrance.

• Avoid keeping students in your classroom for long periods of time after dismissal.

• Particularly with respect to pre-adolescent and adolescent students, when disciplining them or discussing a contentious issue, (e.g., a student's grade on an assignment) call in another teacher to witness the discussion or do it quietly while other students are present.

• Do not go behind tall room dividers or tall freestanding bookshelves with a single student.

• Do not go into photography dark rooms, small physical education rooms off the gymnasium, concealed cloakrooms or storage rooms with a single student.

• If you have a window in your door, do not cover it up.

• Where possible, schools should be designed or redesigned so that office administrators have one glass wall which is in easy view of the secretarial staff yet sufficiently private from the view of other students or visitors to the school.

• Love for children implies respect for their privacy. Show your love by listening to them, being verbally supportive and understanding and treating them fairly. Save physical demonstrations of caring and affection for when you are in public view of other students or teachers.

• Beware of pre-adolescent and adolescent students who seem to find you attractive. Subdue the flattery. Cool the attention. Avoid and discourage teasing. Remember the danger of a lover spurned, real or imaginary.

• Encourage emotional growth and independence in students. If too many children are clinging to your pant legs, beware. The power you have over an emotionally dependent student puts you at an unfair advantage over that student and may elicit irrational responses if that power is not exercised with extreme caution.

• "Huggy Bears" are particularly vulnerable to accusations of physical impropriety with students. Consider whether all that touching makes you feel good or is it for the benefit of students.

• Where physical affection is appropriate, keep your hands above the student's lower body and chest area. Avoid the friendly pat on the butt, even with very young children, and do not under any but necessary circumstances (i.e., injury of a young child) hold students on your lap.

• Remember that the role of a teacher acting *in loco parentis* does not equate to the role of a parent. That doctrine places teachers in place of parents for the purpose of educating children and caring for them during school sponsored activity. It does not entitle teachers to the same degree of physical intimacy with students as is shared between children and their parents.

• Principals and teachers must be alert to colleagues whose overly affectionate manner may leave them vulnerable to accusations of physical impropriety and should provide such individuals with necessary cautions and counseling.

(Doctor, 1999, pp. 12-13)

Conclusion

In an age when sexual misconduct appears to be rampant, it is imperative that teachers and school administrators be highly cognizant of their interactions with students which could be misconstrued as having sexual intentions. As stated several times already in this text, there is always a concern when dealing with matters of a legal nature that teachers and school administrators become paranoid. The resultant danger from such paranoia is that students are not dealt with in the caring and nurturing manner that has come to be expected from educators. Common sense and a reasonable modicum of caution should prevail and thus students are afforded the degree of professionalism they deserve.

For Discussion

1. The topic of sexual assault is one that can create paranoia in any one working with children, no matter what the age. What age/grade levels would you perceive to be the most problematic for teachers? Why this particular age/grade level?

2. This whole issue of "touch" is significant in education but one that can cause problems for teachers. What advice would you pass onto teachers at the following grade levels:

a) primary (kindergarten to grade 3);

b) elementary (grades 4 to 6);

c) junior high (grades 7 to 9); and

d) senior high (grades 10 to 12)?

9

Duty to Report

Across Canada all provinces have legislation designed to protect children. This legislation is independent of education or school acts but obviously impacts on how we interact with children in the delivery of educational services. This chapter will focus on that aspect of all provincial child welfare legislation which has significant implications for all educators, the requirement of "mandatory reporting" or "duty to report."

Mandatory Reporting Defined

Mandatory reporting refers to a legal or statutory duty requiring any individual who has knowledge or a reasonable suspicion that a child is in need of protection to report such a matter to the appropriate authorities such as the Director of Child Welfare or a peace officer. In practice, these reports are usually made to a social worker or to a police officer. Section 22 of the *Child Protection Act of Prince Edward Island* (1988) is an example of this requirement and reads as follows:

2. (1) Notwithstanding any other Act, every person who has knowledge or has reasonable grounds to suspect that a child is in need of protection shall

(a) without delay, report or cause to be reported the circumstances to the Director, or to a peace officer who shall report the information to the Director; and

(b) provide to the Director such additional information as is known or available to the person.

(2) Subsection (1) applies notwithstanding the confidential nature of the information on which the report is based, but nothing in this section abrogates any solicitor-client privilege.

(3) Subject to subsection (5), no person shall reveal or be compelled to reveal the identity of a person who has made a report or provided information respecting a child pursuant to subsection (1).

(4) Subject to subsection (5), a person who makes a report or provides information pursuant to subsection (1) or who does anything to assist in an investigation carried out by the Director is not liable to any civil action in respect of providing such information or assistance.

(5) Subsections (3) and (4) do not apply where a person knowingly makes a report or provides information which is false or misleading.

2000(2nd),c.3,s.22.

(http://www.canlii.org/pe/laws/sta/c-5.1/20060518/whole.html)

In some provinces the term "duty to report" is quite commonly used. Synonymous with the term "mandatory reporting," the term "duty to report" is actually used in the child protection legislation in several provinces.

Three underlying principles guide the mandatory reporting laws:

1. reporting statutes or laws were designed to expedite identification of abused children by the child protection system;

2. these statutes designated specific agencies to receive, investigate and manage cases of maltreatment; and

3. reporting statutes were intended to prevent further abuse and to help preserve family unity and welfare (Dove, Miller, & Miller, 2003, p. 23).

Whether or not this duty to report has lived up to these various expectations is somewhat debatable.

Challenges for Teachers and Administrators

Research conducted by O'Toole, Webster, O'Toole and Lucal (1999) on teachers' recognition and the reporting of child abuse suggests that the incidences of reporting are directly related to the characteristics of (a) the case, (b) the teacher, and (c) the educational setting. They concluded that teachers' responses to child abuse are relatively unbiased by either the extraneous characteristics of the perpetrator or the victim, the responding teacher, or the school setting. However, these researchers determined that there is evidence for under-reporting particularly in less serious cases involving physical and emotional abuse (p. 1083).

A study by Kenny (2001) examined teachers' perceived deterrents to reporting of child abuse. Most of the teachers stated that they would report the abuse to their school administration, but also stated previously that their administration would not support them if they made child abuse reports. When teachers defer this responsibility, the researcher determined that the abuse is less likely to be reported and more likely to continue, thus placing the child at risk for continued abuse. There also appears to be a diffusion of responsibility, whereby teachers may feel that someone else (i.e., counsellor, principal) is responsible for reporting the abuse.

These findings were consistent with other research (e.g., James & DeVaney, 1994) that found that school professionals are reluctant to report child abuse violations, especially by members of their staff (i.e., other teachers). The most commonly cited reason for failure to report this abuse was fear of making an inaccurate report, followed by feeling as though child protective services does not offer help to maltreated children. It seems that the fear of making a false report outweighs the desire to follow legal standards in protecting children. This suggests that there is a need for educating teachers about child abuse reporting. In these instances, both of which were reportable, most teachers failed to respond.

Perhaps the major challenge for education practitioners is knowing when they should report suspicions of child abuse. This whole area is one permeated by a considerable degree of "grey" and is one that education practitioners agonize over. Levin and Young (2002) raise several questions and concerns worth considering:

> For instance, what constitutes a strong enough suspicion to justify reporting a suspected case of abuse? After all, many of the possible symptoms of abuse, especially in regard to emotional abuse or neglect, might be found in most children at one time or another. What if a child does not want to have the abuse reported for fear that the family will be torn apart by an accusation? What if the report is made, but there is not enough evidence to warrant criminal charges? (This is a real concern with child abuse since the sole evidence for the allegation may be the unsubstantiated word of a child, which does not have the same force in a court of law as does the testimony of an adult.) What if no charges are laid, but the abusing adult is provoked into greater abuse by the fact that an investigation is being conducted? (pp. 126-127)

Advice for Teachers and Administrators

The literature on reporting child abuse advises teachers and school administrators of the usual legal points they need to be aware of:

1. You are required by law to report your suspicion of abuse, even if you do not have any concrete evidence to support your belief.

2. You must make a report to the legally stipulated authority, usually the police, or to the child welfare authorities; reporting only to your principal is not sufficient.

3. You can be found guilty of a crime if you have knowledge or suspicion of abuse and do not report it to the proper authorities.

4. Your identity will not be disclosed to the person who is suspected of committing the abuse.

5. You cannot be punished or prosecuted for making a report that proves to be incorrect, as long as you did so in good faith. (Young & Leven, 2002, p. 126)

Teachers and school administrators exercise professional judgment and discretion on a consistently regular basis. This area involving the duty to report is, for the various reasons cited earlier, one that is particularly troubling and perhaps requisite of the wisdom of Solomon! For teachers it is recommended that they consult with their school administrator and guidance counselor; a consult with a social worker might also be advisable. School districts usually employ educational psychologists and discussing the situation with these professionals might also be helpful. For school administrators, the same suggestions are suggested. It should be kept in mind of course that consultations serve as advisory in nature and the bottom line is that it is the teacher or the school administrator who must make the decision to report or not to report.

Conclusion

This statutory duty to report any suspicions of child abuse is one that has come about as a result of significant harm to children over the years, whether it be in an educational setting or at home. It is therefore understandable why we have such legislation to protect children. However, the reality is that this legislation causes practitioners in education considerable worry and stress. The professions of teaching and school administration carry with them serious responsibilities and the duty to report is one of those responsibilities. At the end of the day if the practitioner has consulted with the appropriate individuals and given much thought to the desired course of action and then makes a decision, then s/he has lived up to the expectations of the profession and the law. That is all that can be expected.

For Discussion

1. Are teachers in general aware of their responsibility to report suspicions of child abuse? Discuss.

2. Discuss the various factors teachers need to consider when faced with the possibility they may suspect child abuse.

3. Although the duty to report legislation could be characterized as "black and white," should such legislation be less so for a variety of reasons? Discuss.

10

The Youth Criminal Justice Act

Teachers and school administrators working in junior and senior high schools invariably come into contact with youth who have run afoul of the legal system. These students fall under the jurisdiction of the *Youth Criminal Justice Act* (YCJA) which replaced the controversial *Young Offenders Act* (YOA) as of April 1, 2003.

This chapter will, in addition to giving an overview of the background and philosophy of the YCJA, consider a number of issues confronting teachers and school administrators in their involvement with the youth justice system.

Background

Canada has a long history of enacting legislation to deal with youth crime. *The Juvenile Delinquents Act* (JDA) was introduced in 1908 with the court playing "the role of a judicial parent in determining whether a young person should be deemed a delinquent" (Tustin & Lutes, 2004, p. 1). Tustin and Lutes further add that

> Young people were not given the benefit of legal representation, and the information brought before the court was often based on hearsay. Once the court deemed the youth to be a juvenile delinquent, the court could order the young person to a training school until the authorities felt the youth should be released. The state took over the role of the parent and made all decisions regarding physical care, education and contact with family members. Future plans for the youth rested with the training school and the probation officer. (p. 1)

This legislation remained in force until 1984 when it was replaced by the *Young Offenders Act*. The thinking behind the YOA was radically different:

> It was the beginning of a new approach, where youths were given the right to due process, and youths and their parents were expected to be accountable. It was a drastic change in the way youth justice had worked. The age in which a young person could be charged was raised from seven to a minimum of 12 and a maximum of 17. Each and every young person was rep-

resented in court by legal counsel, and the courts were expected to protect a young person's rights. The police had to follow the technical procedures of the Act to the letter when laying a charge, or the charge would not proceed. (Tustin & Lutes, 2004, p. 1)

Although the YOA attempted to establish a tighter legal framework for dealing with youth crime, it soon became very controversial. According to Payne (2006), "the most significant problems were the vagueness and inconsistency of both the principles within the Act and their implementation" (p. 12). Carrington and Schulenburg (2005) speak to those inconsistencies:

The YOA provided police and other decision-makers with a set of principles that were, according to one authority, "not coherent and, in some instances, . . . positively inconsistent" (Platt, 1991) and [provided] practically no guidance on how to resolve its apparent inconsistencies in making decisions under its authority. (Section 1.1)

A complicated piece of legislation that was often misunderstood, the YOA, instead of promoting the use of diversionary programs to keep young people out of custody, did the opposite – it increased the use of custody to the point whereby Canada had the highest rate of youth incarceration in the western world (Tustin & Lutes, 2004). As a result of criticism of the YOA escalating to the point where there was a serious lack of public confidence in the youth justice system, the federal government launched a review of the Act. This review resulted in the creation and passage of the *Youth Criminal Justice Act in* 2003.

Principles Underpinning the YCJA

According to Weir (2003), the YCJA is an attempt by the federal government to reconcile two competing views of youth crime:

1. On one hand, a few highly publicized crimes have created a public perception that youth crime is increasing and young people are out of control. In this perception, the YOA has created a justice system that is soft on young people and does not adequately address victim's rights.

2. On the other hand, the reality is that Canada is tougher on youth crime than most other comparable countries. Canada has the highest youth incarceration rate of any country in the western world, including the United States. Most of the young people who are incarcerated are imprisoned for crimes related to property. Only 20% of young people in custody in Canada have committed violent offences. In fact, the youth incarceration rate is higher than the adult incarceration rate in Canada and young people often receive longer sentences than adults for similar offences. (p. 1)

Section 3 of the YCJA is referred to as the "Declaration of Principle" and lists the major principles underpinning the philosophy of the act. According to Barnhorst (2004), the YCJA

> emphasizes restraint, accountability, proportionality, and greater structuring of the discretion of decision makers. It contains provisions to encourage the use of extrajudicial measures, including a presumption that nonviolent first offenders should be dealt with through extrajudicial measures. Conferences are recognized as a potentially useful means of improving decision making. Pre-trial detention is prohibited for child welfare purposes and presumed to be unnecessary if the youth could not be sentenced to custody. The sentencing principles set out a new approach to sentencing. Sentences must be proportionate to the seriousness of the offence and, within the limits of proportionality, must promote rehabilitation. The sentencing provisions also place specific restrictions on the use of custody. (p. 231)

Although these principles stated above are probably perceived as "motherhood" by most of us, there are some challenges with this new act. However, those challenges associated with the YCJA would appear to involve its operationalization on a daily basis – that is, how the act is interpreted and used on a daily basis by those who are involved with young offenders – the police, the court system, educators and the like. One of the strong points of the YCJA is that, compared to the YOA, there is much greater direction given, thus decreasing the degree of individual interpretation and subjectivity. To date, from a number of discussions the author has had with practitioners in the youth justice system (i.e., youth court workers), perceptions of the utility and the effectiveness of the YCJA are highly positive, a contrast indeed to those of the earlier YOA.

Significance for the School System

There are times when school administrators and teachers come into direct contact with young offenders. These young offenders may be in open or secure custody arrangements. Open custody refers to a placement in a group home whereas secure custody would involve living in a residential institution for young offenders. Generally, these residential institutions would have their own facilities and teachers for educating the youth offenders. In open custody situations the offenders would be enrolled as a student in a nearby school.

One of the issues school administrators and teachers experienced with the YOA was the secrecy surrounding the nature of the conduct which resulted in the youth being placed into open custody. Youth court workers tended to be tight-lipped on that subject because of their interpretation of the confidentiality clause in the YOA. The school administrator has a statutory duty to provide a safe and secure environment to students and this issue arises when s/he is concerned, as a result of a youth offender or offenders being placed in the school, that the school's safety and security might be compromised.

The YCJA addresses this concern with a section that speaks directly to this very issue. Section 126, subsection 6 of the act states:

> The provincial director, a youth worker, the Attorney General, a peace officer or any other person engaged in the provision of services to young persons may disclose to any professional or other person engaged in the supervision or care of a young person – including a representative of any school board or school or any educational or training institution – any information contained in a record kept under sections 114 – 116 if the disclosure is necessary
>
> a. to ensure compliance by the young person with an authorization under section 91 or an order on the youth justice court;
>
> b. to ensure the safety of staff, students or other persons; or
>
> c. to facilitate the rehabilitation of the young person.

Subsection 7 of the YCJA places some restrictions on the use of that information:

> A person to whom information is disclosed under subsection 6 shall
>
> a. keep the information separate from any other record of the young person to whom the information relates;
>
> b. ensure that no other person has access to the information except if authorized under this Act, or if necessary for the purposes of subsection 6; and
>
> c. destroy their copy of the record when the information is no longer required for the purpose for which it was disclosed.

It has also been the author's personal experience that young offenders in general tend to be most co-operative and compliant in the regular school setting. There may be several reasons for this, such as their realizing that they may have sanctions imposed on them in the residential setting and that a lack of co-operation/compliance might negatively impact on their release time. An open line of communication between the school and the youth workers is essential if the school experience is to be a positive and productive one for the young offender.

Other Issues in the School Setting

Shortly after the YCJA came into effect, a symposium was hosted by the Ontario Principals' Council titled "Student Offenders: The intersection of the YCJA and Schools" (Ontario Principals' Council, 2004, p. 6). Some of the issues explored in that symposium included the following:

• when the school principal should call the police;

• the status of the principal's inquiry as required by the [Ontario] Education Act vs. police investigations;

• the conflict between the principal's role as witness in police interviews vs. the principal's role as investigator when conducting an enquiry under the [Ontario] Education Act;

• when charges or diversion should be used.

The top three issues identified in this symposium were the following:

1. lack of long-term funding: e.g., for extrajudicial measures, rehabilitation, programs and alternative locations for students on long-term suspensions or expulsion;

2. communication and disclosure issues: schools, in particular, were unsure what information they could get from police and what information they could provide to parents, and the timing of such disclosures; and

3. incongruity between the YCJA and the Education Act. (Ontario Principals' Council, 2004, pp. 6-7)

These comments were made approximately one year after the YCJA came into effect. One major improvement that came with the YCJA, as compared to the YOA, was that the YCJA came with much more direction and guidance regarding its implementation. As mentioned earlier, a primary criticism of the YOA was that it left too much to the discretion of those implementing that piece of legislation. Hopefully, with sufficient time for successful implementation, a number of these issues have been addressed.

Confidentiality and Privacy

Another issue worthy of note involves the teacher or school administrator being called upon by a young person to serve as an advocate for him/her. Section 146(2) of the YCJA allows for a young person, prior to being questioned by police or before giving a statement, to consult a parent or another appropriate person. This appropriate person could be a teacher or school administrator whom the student trusts. In this role the teacher or school administrator may be tempted to ask the student about the specific details of the incident in question. The teacher or school administrator may erroneously think that such information received from the student is privileged meaning confidential and private. However, under Section 146(9) of the YCJA communications between the student and the adult are not protected by any privilege as they would be in a student-lawyer relationship. The adult can be subpoenaed to testify and thus reveal the contents of any discussion between the student and him/her.

The best advice a teacher or school administrator could offer in this situation is not to give any legal advice except to advise the student to contact a lawyer. Where lack of financial resources is an issue, the student in question should be referred to the local legal aid office.

Conclusion

Although the YCJA has only been in use for a little over four years, there are indications that this legislation is making progress in achieving the goals as set out by the federal parliament of Canada. Literature in the field of criminal justice which gives significant insight into the day to day workings and both the positives and negatives of this relatively new legislation is beginning to emerge (e.g., Barnhorst, 2004; Carrington & Schulenberg, 2004; Harris, Weagant, Cole & Weinper, 2004; Pulis & Sprott, 2005). This information should prove to be of tremendous help to those who work on an every day basis with the YCJA.

Granted, "the jury is still out," but all indications are that the YCJA is a significant improvement over the YOA. Over the next several years, teachers and school administrators will continue to have greater involvement with young offenders. It is incumbent upon all of us in education to give this legislation the appropriate time and latitude to be successful.

For Discussion

1. What has been your personal experience as an educator dealing with young offenders? Elaborate.

2. List any specific issues you perceive to be of significance when discussing young offenders and their education. Elaborate.

3. What is your own philosophy with respect to working with young offenders in the classroom?

4. a. What perceptions currently exist in your community regarding young offenders in general and specifically, young offenders in the regular school system?

   b. In your opinion are these perceptions accurate and/or valid? Elaborate.

5. Are there specific strategies (pedagogical or otherwise) that you might utilize in working with young offenders in your classroom? Elaborate.

11

Teachers' Codes of Ethics

The various teachers' associations across Canada have developed codes of ethics or codes of professional conduct/practice for its members. These codes serve a number of functions:

1. to enlighten teachers as to the various ethics central to their profession;

2. to provide teachers with a guide for their professional practice;

3. to inspire teachers to live up to that guide on a daily basis;

4. to highlight and emphasize teachers' responsibilities to their students, colleagues and other stakeholders in education.

This chapter will examine various sections common in codes of ethics as well as highlighting various concerns related to the practical aspects of those codes. For an actual sample of a teachers' code of ethics, see Appendix B of this publication.

Commonalities

An examination of various teachers' codes of ethics across Canada and indeed around the world reveals a number of common themes permeating the text of those codes. Generally, these themes, with some exceptions, focus on the teacher's responsibilities to

- students;
- his/her employer, most often the school board;
- colleagues (fellow teachers and administrators);
- parents;
- his/her professional development; and
- his/her professional organization.

Qualities inherent in those themes are care, trust, respect and integrity.

Students

Teachers' codes of ethics routinely speak to the ethical conduct towards students and as referenced by the Association of American Educators (AAE) (www.aaeteachers.org/code-ethics.shtml), state that ." . . all educators are obligated to help foster civic virtues such as integrity, diligence, responsibility, cooperation, loyalty, fidelity, and respect for the law, for human life, for others and for self."

The Newfoundland and Labrador Teachers' Association lists the following "tenets" in its code of ethics section on teacher-pupils:

1. A teacher's first responsibility is to the enhancement of the quality of education provided to the pupils in his/her charge.

2. A teacher regards as confidential, and does not divulge, other than to appropriate persons, any information of a personal or domestic nature concerning either pupils or their homes.

3. A teacher keeps teaching as objective as possible in discussing with the class the controversial matters whether political, religious or racial.

4. A teacher does not knowingly misuse professional position for personal profit in the offering of goods or services to pupils or to their parents.

5. A teacher does not accept pay for tutoring his/her own pupils in the subject in which the teacher gives classroom instruction.

6. A teacher accepts that the intellectual, moral, physical and social welfare of his/her pupils is the chief aim and end of education.

7. A teacher recognizes that a privileged relationship exists between the teacher and his/her pupils and shall never exploit this relationship.

8. A teacher who has reason to suspect that a child has suffered, or is suffering, from abuse that may have been caused or permitted by any person shall forthright report the suspected abuse to the appropriate authorities. (www.nlta.nl.ca)

All of the various statements as articulated by the AAE are embodied in these various tenets.

Employer

Section IV of the *Nova Scotia Teachers' Union Code of Ethics* focuses on teachers' relationships to the "external administration" (i.e., school board):

a. The teacher should adhere to a contract until the contract has been terminated by mutual consent, or the contract has otherwise been legally terminated. A verbal agreement is a contract.

b. The teacher should not accept a salary below that which s/he would receive according to the scale negotiated between the Nova Scotia Teachers' Union (NSTU) and the school board.

c. The teacher should not accept a salary above that which s/he would receive according to the scale negotiated between the Nova Scotia Teachers' Union and the school board, without notifying the Local of the NSTU. (www.nstu.ca)

Sections of codes of ethics/professional conduct dealing with the employer are in the minority across Canada. Newfoundland and Labrador, Nova Scotia and Alberta appear to make up that minority. The themes of collective agreements, contracts and salaries dominate those sections.

Colleagues

This section is a major part of codes of ethics across the country. This section in the Alberta Teachers' Association (ATA) Code of Professional Conduct is highly typical:

12. The teacher does not undermine the confidence of pupils in other teachers.

13. The teacher criticizes the professional competence or professional reputation of another teacher only in confidence to proper officials and after the other teacher has been informed of the criticism, subject only to Section 24 of the *[Alberta] Teaching Profession Act.*

14. The teacher, when making a report on the professional performance of another teacher, does so in good faith and, prior to submitting the report, provides a copy of the report, subject only to section 24 of the *[Alberta] Teaching Profession Act.*

15. The teacher does not take, because of animosity or for personal advantage, any steps to secure the dismissal of another teacher.

16. The teacher recognizes the duty to protest through proper channels administrative policies and practices which the teacher cannot in conscience accept; and further recognizes that if administration by consent fails, the administrator must adopt a position of authority.

17. The teacher as an administrator provides opportunities for staff members to express their opinions and to bring forth suggestions regarding the administration of the school. (www.teachers.ab.ca)

Parents

This particular category is not always directly included in codes of ethics. However, where it is, the theme of co-operation stands out:

(i) A teacher seeks to establish friendly and co-operative relationships with the home and to provide parents with information that will serve the best interests of their children. (Newfoundland and Labrador Teachers' Association Code of Ethics)

In codes where there is no specific section dedicated to parents, it is subsumed under various other categories such as that of "trust" in the Ontario College of Teachers' statement on "The Ethical Standards for the Teaching Profession":

The ethical standard of Trust embodies fairness, openness and honesty. Members' professional relationships with students, colleagues, parents, guardians and the public are based on trust.

Professional Development

This category is understandably a significant aspect of most codes of ethics. Although it may not be listed as a separate topic in various codes, it too is usually subsumed under a number of different headings. The Saskatchewan Teachers' Code of Ethics contains 21 articles and a number of those speak to professional development both directly and indirectly:

• Article 3: Promotion of Teaching – To make the teaching profession attractive in ideals and practices so that people will desire to enter it.

• Article 8: Competence to Teach – To strive to be competent in the performance of any teaching services that are undertaken on behalf of students, taking into consideration the context and circumstances for teaching.

• Article 10: Recognition of Diversity in Education – To develop teaching practices that recognize and accommodate diversity within the classroom, the school and the community.

• Article 12: Commitment to Student Development – To encourage each student to reach the highest level of individual development.

• Article 13: Improvement of Teaching and Learning – To seek to meet the needs of students by designing the most appropriate learning experiences for them.

• Article 14: Mediation of the Curriculum – To implement the provincial curriculum conscientiously and diligently, taking into account the context for teaching and learning provided by students, the school and the community.

• Article 21: Improvement of Educational Policies – To seek to be aware of the need for changes in local association, Federation, school, school division and Department of Learning policies and regulations. (www.stf.sk.ca)

Professional Organization

It is understandable that teachers' codes of ethics, because they are generally developed by professional associations, would have a section devoted to the ethical behavior of teachers towards the organization itself. The *Code of Ethics of the Northwest Territories Teachers' Association* does exactly that:

• It is the right and responsibility of members to participate in, be informed of and inform themselves of Association business and, where appropriate, to make such informed criticisms as the facts appear to warrant.

• Members of the Association shall not, as an individual or as a member of a group of teachers, make unauthorized representations to employers or outside bodies in the name of the Association or in the name of a Local Association or Regional Association.

• Members of the Association shall acknowledge and respect the authority and responsibilities of the Association and its officers, and shall not conduct themselves in a manner prejudicial to the collective bargaining strategies or other interests of the Association.

• Members of the Association shall co-operate with the Association in connection with the investigation of all complaints of professional misconduct.

• Members of the Association shall co-operate with the association in connection with the investigation and processing of grievances under the collective agreement, and shall honor commitments in that regard made on their behalf by the Association.

• Members of the Association shall endeavor to maintain a harmonious and mutually beneficial relationship with the Association.

(www.nwtta.nt.ca)

A Concern From the Field

One of the concerns that the author has experienced as a high school principal involved several examples of a teacher "bullying" a fellow teacher. Such bullying or teacher abuse does happen and is what Hoyle (1986) refers to as "the dark side of organizational life" in schools and school districts (p. 87).

The author's experience was such that teachers would inform him about specific incidents whereby they were undermined to the point of embarrassment by a colleague in front of students. These teachers were advised that under our code of ethics they were expected to approach the colleague in question and discuss the specific concern. However, the response from the teachers was that they were physically intimidated and frightened by this particular colleague and that they had a legitimate concern regarding their personal safety if that course of action was followed. This situation obviously begs the question as to whether or not a teacher should be allowed to "hide behind the code of ethics."

Teachers should not be able to hide behind the code of ethics and one would hope that such methods of avoiding the truth were not a part of the thinking that went into developing codes of ethics. Coombs (2005) addresses this issue:

> Know your rights! Get the facts before conceding or challenging. Engage support. Check with someone before responding. If you have concerns about insubordination, call the NLTA [your association] for information or advice. The Code of Ethics for Teachers requires you to confront a colleague before going to a superior about issues, yet it is unreasonable to expect a teacher to confront someone who is already a personal threat. Therefore, written concerns can be delivered to the colleague explaining that a personal confrontation would be counterproductive and these concerns will go to another level for consideration and intervention. (p. 18)

This is very sage advice and when in doubt regarding such matters as these, teachers should always approach their school administrators and "in confidence" ask for guidance as to how to handle these complicated matters. School administrators, by the very nature of the position they hold, have a wealth of knowledge about personnel matters and in all probability have had firsthand experience in situations similar to the one discussed above.

Conclusion

This chapter has focused on the philosophy and the utility of teachers' codes of ethics. Although the wording of these codes may vary from jurisdiction to jurisdiction, they have many commonalities. These are insightful documents and, although somewhat idealistic, serve a very useful function in giving us guidance as to how we conduct ourselves as teachers and school administrators.

For Discussion

1. In addition to the various themes permeating teachers' codes of ethics discussed above, are there additional themes/categories that should be covered in these codes? Elaborate on why you have chosen these particular ones.

2. Colleagues bullying colleagues. Discuss how you might deal with such a situation.

3. What do you perceive to be the value, if any, of teachers' codes of ethics? Elaborate.

4. Should teachers' codes of ethics have a category dealing with their professional associations? Elaborate.

12

Copyright Law

In recent years there has been considerable discussion among educators as to what copyright is all about. This chapter will take a look at what the copyright law says and the various rules and regulations that teachers and school administrators need to be aware of in their everyday work in the classroom.

Copyright Defined

According to Harris (2001), the purpose of copyright is to "give copyright holders control over the use of their creations" (p. 3). Copyright protects original literary, artistic, musical and dramatic works. The Canadian Intellectual Property Office (2007) summarizes copyright as follows:

In the simplest terms, "copyright" means "the right to copy." Only the owner of copyright, very often the creator of the work, is allowed to produce or reproduce the work in question or to permit anyone else to do so. Suppose, for example, that you have written a novel. Copyright law rewards and protects your creative endeavor by giving you the sole right to publish or use your work in any number of ways. You may also choose not to publish your work and to prevent anyone else from doing so. (p. 1)

Federal Legislation

In Canada copyright is regulated by federal legislation referred to as the *Copyright Act* first enacted in 1921. Over the years with the rapid technological changes having a major impact on the production of creative works, there have been numerous changes to the act. In 1988 a significant revision of the act occurred in an attempt to address some of the issues dealing with technology. A further revision took place in 1997 resulting in several new regulations regarding sound recordings.

Copyright in Schools

There is a preponderance of practical information on copyright written for educational institutions. Perhaps the most complete and up-to-date source of information is the federal government's Canadian Intellectual Property Office (CIPO) web-site. Much of the information cited in this chapter has been taken from that web-site.

The CIPO provides a rationale which allows for exceptions to copyright legislation applicable to educational institutions:

> An exception permits the use of a work protected by copyright without the consent of the copyright owner and without the payment of royalties. Copyright laws all over the world aim for a balance between a) the rights of creators to be paid for and to control the use of their works; and b) the needs of users who want access to material protected by copyright. This balance is created by providing creators with legal "rights" and then limiting those rights through "exceptions" for the benefit of certain users. Educational institutions are one of those user groups [and various sections of the Act] provide educational institutions with exceptions defining certain activities which may be undertaken without infringing copyright. (http://strategis.ic.gc.ca/sc_mrksv/cipo/cp/cp_circ_12-e.html)

Specific Exceptions

The concept of fair dealing is one that teachers should be aware of when using copyrighted material. MacKay and Sutherland (2006) state that fair dealing means "a teacher can copy a small portion of a work without infringing copyright, but they must be careful to limit the portion as much as possible" (p. 198).

Performance of Musical Works

Section 27(3) of the Copyright Act states that

> an educational institution is not required to pay any royalties for the public performance of any musical work "in furtherance of an educational object." For example, performance of music in class for the purpose of giving music instruction falls within this exception. However, the exception excludes the use of music for non-educational objects such as dances, school concerts, or as background music. This means that music used at school concerts, assemblies, or school dances must be paid for through tariffs administered by a performing rights society called SOCAN because those events are not "in furtherance of an educational object."

Right of Reproduction

Section 29.4 is an exception to the right of reproduction:

This exception allows copying onto a blackboard, a flip chart or other similar display devices in the classroom. Educational institutions are also permitted to copy materials onto transparencies. Copying works protected by copyright for tests or examinations is another permitted use. These exceptions apply unless the work is "commercially available" in a form which meets the educator's needs. "Commercially available" is defined (in Section 2) as meaning available on the Canadian market within a reasonable time, for a reasonable price and with reasonable effort or is available through a licence from a collective society.

Public Performances

Subsections 29.5, 29.6 and 29.7 allow for exceptions to a copyright owner's exclusive right of public performance:

Subsection 29.5 permits non-profit educational institutions to have live performances on school premises and to play sound recordings, radios and televisions on school premises. Subsection 29.6 permits non-profit educational institutions to reproduce and perform, on their premises, news and commentary from radio and television programs for educational purposes. However, the proposed exception is subject to certain conditions:

1. A copy can be made and shown, without authorization or payment, an unlimited number of times for a period of up to one year from the date of the taping.

2. After the year is over, copied materials, must either be erased or the copyright owner notified.

3. The Copyright Board, a specialized tribunal under the Copyright Act, would then set a royalty or fee for the reproduction and each subsequent performance of the copied material for educational purposes.

4. Subsection 29.7 permits all other types of broadcast programs to be reproduced without permission and examined for up to 30 days in order to decide whether the copy will be used on school premises, for educational purposes.

5. If these other types of broadcast programs are used, then a royalty, set by the Copyright Board for the reproduction and each subsequent use of the copy, must be paid for by non-profit educational institutions.

Publication of Literary Works

Section 30 of the Act permits publication of short passages from literary works for schools. This particular exception has many conditions that must be met before it applies:

1. The publication must be composed primarily of non-copyright material.

2. The collection must be intended for the use of schools.

3. What is reproduced must be from short passages of published literary works.

4. Those short passages must not have been published for use by schools.

5. Not more than two passages from works by the same author can be reproduced by the same publisher within five years.

6. The source from which the passages are taken must be acknowledged.

7. The name of the author, if given in the source, is mentioned.

Educators' Use of Print Materials

Educators commonly use photocopied material to supplement prescribed instructional materials in their classrooms. All publicly funded schools in the K-12 school systems across Canada are covered by a license with Access Copyright. Each province and territory pay annual fees to Access Copyright for this licence; these fees are then distributed to copyright owners.

Noel (2005) further explains:

The Access Copyright license provides permission to educational institutions to make reprographic copies, the most common form of which are photocopies. The Access Copyright licence also provides teachers and students with limited rights to copy legally the published print works of others without seeking permission. But the licence does not give teachers and students the right to do any and all forms of reproduction. (p. 7)

Teachers and students are allowed to make photocopies for school purposes, including class sets, as well as for administration, communications with parents, and library use. Under the Access Copyright licence up to 10 per cent of a work may be photocopied. More than 10 per cent may be copied under the following circumstances:

1. a full chapter that constitutes 20 per cent or less of a book;

2. a complete single short story, play, essay, or poem from a book, periodical, or anthology;

3. an entire newspaper article or page;

4. an entry from a reference work;

5. an illustration or photograph from a publication containing other works;

6. large-print material to accommodate the perceptually disabled, published in Canada;

7. in limited cases, as specified in the licence, out-of-print books.

(Noel, 2005, p. 8)

Educators' Use of Video Materials

Whether it is for instructional or motivational reasons, teachers common-ly use videos in their classrooms. How does such use fit into the copyright law? Noel (2005) has this to say:

> A copyright owner has the right to authorize and get paid for the "per-formance in public" of a work, including a video. A Canadian school, under copyright law, is considered to be a public place. In order for a video to be shown in school, it is necessary to have the authorization or permission of the owner of the copyright in the video. A video shown in a school must be cleared for public performance. Videos that are acquired from educational sources or are borrowed from educational media centres will normally include the right to perform the work in public (in a school). Videos that are rented or purchased from most commercial sources such as video stores are licensed for "home use only" – their performance in a classroom would be an infringement of copyright, unless the user is licensed with a collective for this purpose. The two collectives for such a purpose are Audio-Cine Films Inc. and Visual Education Centre (VEC/Criterion). (p. 14)

Conclusion

The foregoing has given an overview of the various copyright rules and regulations that educators should be aware of. Educators in the past have tend-ed to pay little attention to the importance of copyright. However, with the ever-increasing media emphasis being placed on the value of protecting one's intellectual property, educators have a responsibility to respect that value in their classroom work with students. Noel (2005) eloquently sums up that sen-timent:

> Just as you would want to protect anything that you own, creators want to protect their works. Without copyright protection, there would be little incentive to develop new works as there would be no guarantee that the creators would be paid for their work or that the use of their work would be acknowledged when reprinted or reproduced. As students, we were all

taught the value of original thinking and the importance of not plagiarizing the works of others. Since teachers use copyright materials as well as educate the copyright owners and users of tomorrow, they have a unique responsibility to set the right example. (p. 2)

For Discussion

1. Are today's educators cognizant of the importance of copyright? Why or why not?

2. Do today's educators in general honor copyright rules and regulations? Elaborate.

3. Discuss the practical implications of strictly adhering to the various rules and regulations articulated in the Copyright Act.

4. Do you perceive plagiarism to be a problem in the K-12 school system? Elaborate.

5. What strategies might be used to combat incidents of plagiarism in schools?

13

Workplace Safety in Schools

An issue that has been given increasing attention in recent years is that of workplace safety in schools. Precipitated by issues of mold and mildew in classrooms, asbestos insulation in older school buildings and a lack of overall preventative general maintenance, this concern is one that is currently preoccupying parents, teachers, school boards and provincial ministries of education. This issue is particularly acute in provinces struggling to provide school boards with appropriate financial resources for upgrading deficient structures as well as replacing old and outdated buildings.

Workplace safety in schools falls under the umbrella of occupational health and safety legislation and all provinces and territories across Canada have enacted such legislation. In the past schools were not perceived as traditional workplaces but in recent years, due in part to the enthusiasm of the electronic media to aggressively report on those issues alluded to in the previous paragraph, that thinking has changed considerably. The consciousness of school board trustees has been heightened as well to the point where school boards now take vary seriously this whole concept of workplace safety and have followed up with the passage of various policies to ensure that their workers (i.e., students, teachers, support staff) are now safe in their work environment.

Specific Provincial Legislation

The wording and intent is very clear and direct in the provincial legislation on workplace safety. The objectives as outlined in the *Manitoba Workplace Safety and Health Act* (2007) are typical of this legislation across Canada:

2(1) The objects and purposes of this Act are

(a) to secure workers and self-employed persons from risks to their safety, health and welfare arising out of, or in connection with, activities in their workplaces; and

(b) to protect other persons from risks to their safety and health arising out of, or in connection with, activities in workplaces.

Specific objects and purposes

2(2) Without limiting the generality of subsection (1), the objects and purposes of this Act include

(a) the promotion and maintenance of the highest degree of physical, mental and social well-being of workers;

(b) the prevention among workers of ill health caused by their working conditions;

(c) the protection of workers in their employment from factors promoting ill health; and

(d) the placing and maintenance of workers in an occupational environment adapted to their physiological and psychological condition. (www.canlii.org)

According to the *Newfoundland and Labrador Occupational Health and Safety Act* (1990), the employer has a general duty to "ensure, where it is reasonably practicable, the health, safety and welfare of his or her workers" (Section 4). Additionally, the Act goes on to state very specifically what is expected of the employer:

5. Without limiting the generality of section 4, an employer

(a) shall, where it is reasonably practicable, provide and maintain a workplace and the necessary equipment, systems and tools that are safe and without risk to the health of his or her workers;

(b) shall, where it is reasonably practicable, provide the information, instruction, training and supervision and facilities that are necessary to ensure the health, safety and welfare of his or her workers;

(c) shall ensure that his or her workers, and particularly his or her supervisors, are made familiar with health or safety hazards that may be met by them in the workplace;

(d) shall, where it is reasonably practicable, conduct his or her undertaking so that persons not in his or her employ are not exposed to health or safety hazards as a result of the undertaking;

(e) shall ensure that his or her workers are given operating instruction in the use of devices and equipment provided for their protection;

(f) shall consult and co-operate with the occupational health and safety committee, the worker health and safety representative or the workplace health and safety designate, where the employer is not the workplace health and safety designate, on all matters respecting occupational health and safety at the workplace;

(f.1) shall respond in writing within 30 days to a recommendation of

(i) the occupational health and safety committee at the workplace,

(ii) the worker health and safety representative at the workplace, or

(iii) where the employer is not the workplace health and safety designate, the workplace health and safety designate at the workplace

indicating that the recommendation has been accepted or that it has been rejected, with a reason for the rejection;

(f.2) shall provide periodic written updates to

(i) the occupational health and safety committee at the workplace,

(ii) the worker health and safety representative at the workplace, or

(iii) where the employer is not the workplace health and safety designate, the workplace health and safety designate at the workplace

on the implementation of a recommendation accepted by the employer until the implementation is complete;

(f.3) shall consult with

(i) the occupational health and safety committee at the workplace,

(ii) the worker health and safety representative at the workplace, or

(iii) where the employer is not the workplace health and safety designate, the workplace health and safety designate at the workplace

about the scheduling of workplace inspections that are required by the regulations, and ensure that the committee, the worker health and safety representative or the workplace health and safety designate participates in the inspection; and

(g) shall co-operate with a person exercising a duty imposed by this Act or regulations. (www.canlii.org)

The worker also has a legal responsibility to "take reasonable care to protect his or her own health and safety and that of workers and other persons at or near the workplace" (Section 6). As in the case of the employer cited above, the legislation goes on to prescribe specific duties of workers:

7. A worker

(a) shall co-operate with his or her employer and with other workers in the workplace to protect

(i) his or her own health and safety,

(ii) the health and safety of other workers engaged in the work of the employer,

(iii) the health and safety of other workers or persons not engaged in the work of the employer but present at or near the workplace;

(a.1) shall use devices and equipment provided for his or her protection in accordance with the instructions for use and training provided with respect to the devices and equipment;

(b) shall consult and co-operate with the occupational health and safety committee, the worker health and safety representative or the workplace health and safety designate at the workplace; and

(c) shall co-operate with a person exercising a duty imposed by this Act or regulations. (www.canlii.org)

Mention has been made several times in the above legislation to the occupational health and safety committee. Sections 37 and 38 of the *Newfoundland and Labrador Occupational Health and Safety Act* (1990) speak to the purpose and composition of that committee:

37. Where 10 or more workers are employed at a workplace, the employer shall establish an occupational health and safety committee to monitor the health, safety and welfare of the workers employed at the workplace.

38. (1) A committee shall consist of the number of persons that may be agreed to by the employer and the workers but shall not be less than 2 nor more than 12 persons.

(2) At least half of the members of a committee are to be persons representing the workers at the workplace who are not connected with the management of the workplace.

(3) The persons representing the workers on the committee are to be elected by other workers at the workplace or appointed in accordance with the constitution of the union of which the workers are members.

(4) Where the employer and workers cannot agree on the size of the committee, the minister may establish its size.

(5) The employer shall appoint sufficient employer representatives to ensure that the committee may function.

(6) The employer and worker members of a committee shall elect a co-chairperson from their respective groups.

(7) The employer shall post the names of the committee members in a prominent place at the workplace. (www.canlii.org)

Federal Legislation

In 2004 the *Criminal Code of Canada* was amended to include a section devoted to imposing criminal liability for unsafe workplaces. This came about as a result of the 1992 Westray mining disaster in Nova Scotia which claimed the lives of 26 miners. The purpose of this amendment was to encourage a heightened emphasis on safety for workers and the general public by imposing greater liability on employers who show a wanton disregard for the safety of their workers and the public in general.

MacLarkey (2004) summarizes the concerns that school boards should be aware of:

> In the educational context, liability for a school board could arise under section 22.1 where a student, teacher or member of the public is injured by the negligence of a representative, and that negligence could reasonably have been prevented by a senior officer. Where a student is injured arising from the negligence of a representative, the standard against which a senior officer's conduct would be judged is a heightened duty of care. Canadian courts have held that the standard of care owed to a pupil by a school board and its principals and teachers is that of a reasonably careful or prudent parent in the circumstances. Thus, where a senior officer, such as a principal or superintendent, departs markedly from this standard of care, and adherence to this standard of care could have reasonably prevented the harm, such as school yard bullying, the school board employee could be criminally liable. (p. 4)

This amendment also incorporates the rules under currently existing provincial occupational health and safety legislation that exists throughout Canada. Section 217.1 states that

> Everyone who undertakes, or has the authority, to direct how another person does work or performs a task is under a legal duty to take reasonable steps to prevent bodily harm to that person, or any other person, arising from that work or task. (http://laws.justice.gc.ca/en/ShowDoc/cs/c-46//-/en?page=1)

This further strengthens the provisions in the various provincial statutes by incorporating the regulation of health and workplace safety into the *Criminal Code of Canada*. And, should an employer be prosecuted under this federal legislation, the fines levied would be much higher.

School Board Policies

Increasingly, because of both provincial and federal legislation, school boards across Canada are paying greater attention to the issues of occupational health and workplace safety. On the advice of school board lawyers and obviously concerned over the possibility of litigation which could result in stiff financial penalties, school boards have little choice but to take seriously this whole issue of employee safety in the workplace.

Liability and negligence are issues that need to be taken seriously both from a legal and a moral perspective. All indications are that school boards are indeed doing just that.

Conclusion

This chapter has discussed a number of issues and concerns prevalent in workplace health and safety. It is obvious from both the legislation in all provinces and territories now supplemented by the amendment to the federal *Criminal Code of Canada* that governments are taking these issues and concerns very seriously. Although there exists in the provincial and federal legislation a heavy emphasis on the role of the employer, employees have a keen role to play here as well. In the case of schools teachers and administrators need to do their part to ensure that the legislation is practical and workable.

For Discussion

1. Do occupational health and safety committees exist in your place of employment? Comment on their effectiveness.

2. Describe your colleagues' perceptions of these committees.

3. What are some of the issues that your committee has been involved with?

4. Is there a need for these committees? Elaborate.

14

Educational Policy
as a Legal Instrument

Educational policy is a significant part of the lives of teachers and school administrators. More so than ever before, school boards and ministries of education are preoccupied with developing and implementing policies to give direction to the everyday front line work of educators. What is motivating this may have something to do with the litigious society we're living in but the reality is that policy permeates all aspects of the K-12 school system. It is incumbent on today's teachers and school administrators to be knowledgeable of and conversant with, as is reasonably possible, the plethora of policies found on school board websites throughout this country.

This chapter examines the role of these policies as legal instruments. The extent and the degree of the legality of various policies will vary and teachers and school administrators will need to be cognizant of that very aspect as they go about their everyday work as educators.

Policy Defined

Definitions of policy abound but as Cunningham (1963) stated decades ago, "policy is like an elephant – you recognize one when you see it, but it is more difficult to define" (p. 229). This statement is still relevant today. Duke and Canady (1991) concluded that a commonly accepted definition is still missing in both the literature and school practice. A few examples are offered here for your consideration.

Caldwell and Spinks (1988) defined policy as "a statement of purpose and one or more broad guidelines as to how that purpose is to be achieved, which, taken together, provide a framework for the operation of the school or program" (p. 41). They further stated that policy might allow discretion in its implementation, with the basis for that discretion often stated as part of the policy.

Sergiovanni, Burlingame, Coombs and Thurston (1999) referred to policy as "any authoritative communication about how individuals in certain positions should behave under specified conditions" (p. 230). They offer the following examples:

> The principal who issues a memorandum saying that "no teacher should leave the building before 3:45 pm on school days" has fashioned a policy – so has the superintendent who directs principals not to suspend pupils for more than three days without board approval, and the state legislature that enacts a law requiring students to pass a competency test before high school graduation. (p. 230)

"A general approach to things, intended to guide behavior . . . one that has broad implications within a particular setting, whether it be a country, province or school" (pp. 66-67) is how Young and Levin (2002) describe policy. They go on to state that

> Policies shape the structure of schools, the resources available in schools, the curriculum, the teaching staff, and, to a considerable extent, the round of daily activities. Policies determine how much money is spent, by whom and on what, how teachers are paid, how students are evaluated, and most other aspects of schools as we know them. The impact of policies can be illustrated by listing just a few areas of education policy . . . school consolidation, language policy and Aboriginal education. (p. 67)

From these various descriptions of educational policy, it is quite clear that they play a paramount role in the lives of educators.

The Link Between Policy and Legislation

Policies preoccupy the lives of educators and at times keeping a handle on all of these policies can be rather challenging and indeed daunting. This author suggests that there are three levels to these various policies:

• Level 1 – These are policies (not always formally written down) at the school building and classroom level that are somewhat left to the discretion of individual teachers to enforce such as ensuring that there is order and discipline in the classroom to allow for effective teaching. Common sense would dictate that these kinds of policies are there for the good of students but are obviously idiosyncratic to the individual enforcing that specific policy.

The link between these kinds of policies and legislation is a real one in the sense that under provincial education/schools acts teachers and school administrators have a statutory or legal duty to perform those duties articulated in that legislation. However, there is considerable flexibility in how educators might go about enforcing those Level 1 policies.

• Level 2 – These are policies collaboratively developed and then enacted at the school building level which all faculty are expected to enforce and live by on a regular basis. These policies are formally written down and communicated to all students and teachers by the school administration. The flexibility in interpreting and enforcing Level 2 policies is considerably less than Level 1 policies.

The connection between Level 2 policies and legislation is real in the same sense as Level 1 policies. However, these kinds of policies are taken much more seriously by the school administration and teachers are expected to enforce these policies on a regular basis. Failure to do so could result in teachers being issued a reprimand, formal or informal, as such behavior could be perceived as bordering on insubordination. An example of a Level 2 policy might be the banning of cellphones in the classroom.

• Level 3 – These are highly formalized policies emanating from school board offices or ministries of education. Ideally, the development of these policies has been a collaborative process but in practice, that is not always the case. When teachers and school administrators have not been directly involved in the development of these policies, teachers and school administrators may find it rather challenging to "buy into" those policies, thus making the implementation process a "bumpy" one to say the least!

The connection between Level 3 policies and legislation is obviously there as school boards and ministries have a statutory responsibility and right to develop such policies. Highly formalized and usually touted as a positive step forward for education (especially so in the case of policies coming from ministries of education), schools are expected to come on board in enacting and enforcing these policies. An example of a Level 3 policy might be a province-wide safe and caring schools policy.

Schools/Education Acts, Teacher Collective Agreements and Teachers' Codes of Ethics

Specific chapters in this publication have been devoted to schools/education acts, teacher collective agreements and teachers' codes of ethics. These various documents both define the work of teachers and school administrators and prescribe their specific duties. By their very nature, all of these documents have legislative authority and teachers and school administrators can be formally reprimanded if they fail to follow their intent. In a sense these are all policy documents even though we may not think of them in terms of everyday policy.

Conclusion

This chapter has attempted to explain how policy can be interpreted as a legal instrument. The link between legislation and policy is an obvious one but one that teachers and school administrators don't always perceive and appreciate on a daily basis. In the hustle and bustle of everyday school life educators do not have a great amount of time to give serious thought to what some might perceive as rather academic and lofty issues such as educational policy. Suffice it to say that awareness of and some reflection on these issues should hopefully facilitate and not hinder that everyday work.

For Discussion

1. How do educators perceive educational policy? Elaborate.

2. How do educators perceive educational law? Elaborate.

3. Are there any commonalities between educational policy and educational law? Elaborate.

15

Legal versus Moral Dimensions
of Education

In the previous chapters this publication has concentrated on the legal dimensions of education. However, there is another side to education which is highly worthy of consideration – that of the moral dimensions of education. Both of these dimensions co-exist in education and teachers and school administrators need to be cognizant of both dimensions. Although these two dimensions should complement each other, there are times in our work as educators, when they may conflict with each other. Hopefully, this does not happen on a regular basis but when it does, the result is considerable stress and anxiety for those involved.

An analogy that might help to illustrate this dichotomy is the various apartheid conditions that existed in South Africa in pre-Nelson Mandela days. Apartheid was legal in South Africa but in the eyes of blacks and many other groups in that country it was anything but moral. Even though something may be legally correct, one should not necessarily assume that it is always morally right.

This chapter will examine this issue and others and will offer some guidance as to how we as educators might conduct ourselves when these issues arise in our everyday work with students, parents and colleagues.

Specific Issues

Most of the legislation affecting schools should stand up to the scrutiny of the *Charter of Rights and Freedoms* and on a number of occasions, the Supreme Court of Canada has upheld the legality and constitutionality of such legislation (e.g., Section 43 of the *Criminal Code of Canada*).

As discussed in the Chapter 2, section 1 of the Charter speaks to the rights and freedoms that we are all entitled to as Canadians. These rights and freedoms are "subject only to such reasonable limits prescribed by law as can be demonstrably justified in a free and democratic society." Legislation and its attendant regulations are both proactive and reactive meaning that it tells us what can be done and what cannot be done. Legislation and the accompanying regulations impose limits on individual and group behavior. However, these limits, generally speaking, are a necessary aspect of laws.

Special Education

One of the issues the author had to deal with as a high school principal involved a challenging needs student. When that challenging needs student turned 21, s/he could no longer remain in school. Section 3 of the *Newfoundland and Labrador Schools Act* (1997) sets the age range for accessing an education in the K-12 school system from 5 years to 21 years. Legally, the student was being treated correctly but one could make a case that morally, s/he was not being treated properly. The student was living in a community where s/he could not easily access resources and the school was the only institution that could continue to benefit this individual. However, the *Schools Act* was very clear in its Section 3. Here enters that dichotomy alluded to above.

In this case if the parents had the requisite financial resources, they could have obtained legal counsel and perhaps have taken this issue all the way to the Supreme Court of Canada. A possible argument could be made under Section 15.1 of the Charter which deals with equality rights. Specifically, it would appear that this particular individual was being discriminated based on age and mental disability which, under the Charter, is prohibited.

Decision Making in Schools

There are times when teachers and school administrators have to make a choice between what is appropriate legally and what is appropriate morally. These situations often arise in disciplinary matters. Consider a scenario whereby a high school student has stolen several items from the school cafeteria. Upon investigation, the principal is informed that because the student's parents are alcoholics and unable or unwilling to provide for the student, the student is hungry most of the day and this was why s/he stole the items from the cafeteria. Legally, the student did commit theft but is it right morally to turn that student over to the local police station? School administrators face these kinds of issues many times over the course of their careers and one would hope that where possible, they do show empathy and consideration for their students and are able to demonstrate flexibility in their decision making.

In their book, *The Ethics of Teaching,* Strike and Soltis (1992) discuss the dual concepts of consequentialism and non-consequentialism. Simply stated, consequentialism involves making a decision based on the possible consequences of that decision. Conversely, non-consequentialism involves making a decision based on principle without regard for the consequences of that decision. In the everyday work of teachers and school administrators, decisions from these two perspectives are made every day. It is the author's considered opinion that of these two perspectives, consequentialist decision making is the preferred way of making decisions.

In education, teachers and school administrators can often be divided into two camps – the black and white camp and the grey camp. There are individuals who look at life from a black and white perspective, meaning that everything is "cut and dried"; extenuating circumstances are hardly ever, if at all, considered and the specific principle (e.g., honesty, integrity), whatever it is, must be adhered to at all costs! Consequences with respect to whatever decisions are made are not taken into consideration. The author would contend that in schools educators work with individual students and we know that all individuals, students or otherwise, are complex and things are never as simple as they might first appear to be. The author would further contend that life is full of grey and students certainly fit into that categorization. It is suggested that the black and white camp would tend to operate along non-consequentialist lines whereas those in the grey camp would be more consequentialist in their thinking.

Another concept discussed by Strike and Soltis (1992) is benefit maximization. They define benefit maximization as "that, whenever we are faced with a choice, the best and most just decision is the one that results in the most good or the greatest benefit for the most people" (p. 11). There are times that as educators we do make decisions keeping in mind the greater good. An example of this might be a school principal collaborating with the school staff to make a decision regarding students' not being allowed to smoke on school property. Those students who did smoke would obviously be very upset with such a decision but the decision would most definitely be in the best interests of all students including the smokers. One could say that the decision was made for the greater good. Teachers in their classrooms utilize benefit maximization in their decision making on a regular basis. Decisions regarding homework assignments, course projects and classroom management are but a couple of examples of these kinds of decisions.

Conclusion

When thinking about legal issues in education, it is imperative that consideration also be given to the moral perspective of these issues. K-12 educational systems exist to facilitate individuals becoming productive, contributing members of society. That process of individual development (i.e., growing up) is fraught with numerous challenges, some of which will result in our K-12 students making unwise decisions. Enter teachers and school administrators dealing with those decisions and the fallout from those decisions. Depending on the gravity of those unwise decisions, teachers and school administrators will have to take into consideration the various legal and moral perspectives as discussed in this chapter. Consequentialist and non-consequentialist thinking along with the principle of benefit maximization are useful strategies for that consideration.

For Discussion

1. What are some of the legal issues currently being confronted in schools?

2. What are some of the moral issues currently being confronted in schools?

3. Is there any crossover/intersecting of these various issues? Elaborate.

4. In this chapter reference was made to "black and white versus grey." Is this a realistic characterization of a way of thinking on the part of a significant number of educators in the teaching profession? Elaborate.

5. "Consequentialist versus non-consequentialist thinking." Does this accurately represent a way of thinking prevalent in the K-12 school system? Elaborate.

6. Does decision making utilizing the concept of benefit maximization happen in schools? Elaborate.

7. What do you personally think about the concept of benefit maximization?

16

Conclusion

This publication has attempted to give the reader an overview of several of the major legal issues confronting today's teachers and school administrators. The list of issues discussed is not exhaustive but hopefully the information contained in the discussions of those issues will be highly relevant to the everyday work of today's educators.

Determinations and Conclusions

In doing the research for this publication and as a result of the various class discussions in educational law courses both at the undergraduate and graduate levels during the past few years, there are a number of determinations and/or conclusions the author has arrived at. They are presented here for consideration/reflection:

1. *There is a real danger that the information discussed in these chapters can lead to an unnecessary paranoia on the part of teachers and school administrators.*

This is something that teachers and school administrators must resist. Teachers and school administrators have to realize that 99% of time, if they have taken the various precautions in working with students and they have acted as reasonable and responsible educators, they will have done their job the way that is expected of them. This legal information should enable teachers and school administrators, not stifle them.

2. *Reasonableness and respectfulness are the operative words for teachers and school administrators.*

If teachers and school administrators go about their daily work with students and colleagues with these two qualities uppermost in their minds, they will be successful in their efforts. As educators we are role models for our students and it is imperative that we not only talk the talk, but that we also walk the talk! The old adage, "practice what you preach" is perhaps more relevant in today's society, especially so in our teaching, than ever before.

3. *Accidents in schools will happen and do not automatically suggest negligence on the part of teachers and school administrators.*

Because of the litigious society we are living in, it is most important that teachers and school administrators be ever mindful of the possibility that accidents do happen and that they take all reasonable precautions to prevent such accidents from happening.

4. *Teachers and school administrators need to realize that there is a significant amount of grey when dealing with students and colleagues and that life is not all black and white.*

Human beings are complicated and the lives of our students can also be quite complex. It is not always easy for educators to be aware of this but empathy and consideration are laudable qualities in our relationships with others.

5. *With respect to freedom of speech and freedom of expression there are limitations placed on teachers and school administrators.*

There are times when teachers and school administrators, in the course of their work as educators, become very frustrated with their working conditions and they would prefer to voice those concerns in the public domain. However, the reality is that they are not permitted to speak out publicly about such concerns for fear of those remarks being interpreted as an attack on their superiors and therefore of an insubordinate nature. Teachers' codes of ethics and standards for professional conduct require that educators go directly and voice their concerns to those superiors. Whether or not this course of action meets with success is indeed debatable.

6. *When judges make decisions, there is a certain amount of subjectivity in arriving at those decisions.*

Although judges are expected to be one hundred percent objective, one might suggest that true or perfect objectivity can never exist by the very fact that they are human. The context of the specific situation in question, the judge's interpretation of witness accounts, the time in history when the incident occurred – all of these have to enter into the judge's thinking, consciously or subconsciously. Judges have an onerous responsibility and without a doubt strive very diligently to be as objective and impartial as is humanly possible.

7. *Teachers and school administrators are teachers and school administrators 24/7!*

One very important point about the teaching profession is that you are always the teacher or the school administrator. You cannot take that hat off when you leave the school building. Although we often bemoan the fact (if indeed it is a fact) that teachers do not garner the respect and influence that they once had, it is the author's considered opinion that the public still has a considerable amount of respect for teachers. This of course will depend on the particular teacher(s) in a community and the history of teachers in that community and will, for those very reasons, differ from one geographical location to another. Teachers and school administrators are role models and moral exemplars and do have a significant impact (positive or negative) on all of these they come into contact with. As a former president of Harvard University once remarked, "teachers affect eternity"!

8. *It is imperative, albeit challenging, for teachers and school administrators to be knowledgeable of the various legal and moral issues involved in their profession.*

Educators are extremely busy people and there is never enough time in the day (and night) to do all that is required of them. Faculties of education and school districts have a responsibility (one might say "a duty of care") to ensure that teachers and school administrators are pre-serviced and inserviced on these legal and moral issues. Educators need to do their part as well in ensuring that they stay current up-to-date on these issues in their daily practice.

Suggested Sources of Information

There is a widespread misconception that the law is very difficult to keep up-to-date on because it is forever changing at a rapid pace. The reality is that the pace is more of a glacial one and there are ample and very worthwhile resources available to us as educators to keep abreast of the laws that pertain to our profession.

A few of those resources are highly worthy of note. An excellent web site developed by the Canadian Legal Information Institute (www.canlii.org) has a tremendous amount of information which includes all the provincial and federal laws currently in operation throughout the country. Specific judgments (written decisions) including those of the Supreme Court of Canada are also available on this site.

Another organization known as the Canadian Association for the Practical Study of Law in Education (CAPSLE) has a web-site (www.capsle.ca) which allows public access to past issues of its quarterly newsletter, Capsle COMMENTS. This newsletter provides summaries and commentaries on recent cases involving the school systems across Canada.

CAPSLE is a national organization whose aim is to provide an open forum for the practical study of legal issues related to and affecting the education system and its stakeholders. Members include teachers, administrators, board members, trustees, unions, school board associations, educators, academics, students, government and lawyers. CAPSLE is modeled after its American counterpart, the National Organization on Legal Problems in Education (NOLPE).

Another source of excellent legal education information is available from web-sites of the various teacher associations across Canada (e.g. Newfoundland and Labrador Teachers' Association; New Brunswick Teachers' Federation' Alberta Teachers' Association). Google these names to access their web-sites.

A fairly new entity in Canada is the development of colleges of teachers – not to be confused with university-type institutions. Rather, these are agencies established by provincial governments to license, govern and regulate the teaching profession. Two currently exist in Canada, the Ontario College of Teachers and the British Columbia College of Teachers. Their web-sites are also excellent sources of legal education information.

Other very useful sources of legal education information are the provincial departments/ministries of education easily accessed on the world wide web.

Concluding Comments

The study of the legal dimensions of education is both interesting and informative. These dimensions are sometimes perceived as negative, reactive and restrictive but in actuality are positive, proactive and enabling. A knowledge and understanding of these dimensions should greatly facilitate teachers' and school administrators' work with students and colleagues.

APPENDIX A

Canadian Charter of Rights and Freedoms

I✦I Department of Justice   Ministère de la Justice
      Canada   Canada

Schedule B
Constitution Act, 1982

Enacted as Schedule B to the *Canada Act 1982* (U.K.) 1982, c. 11, which came into force on April 17, 1982

PART I
Canadian charter of rights and freedoms

Whereas Canada is founded upon principles that recognize the supremacy of God and the rule of law:

Guarantee of Rights and Freedoms

Rights and
freedoms in
Canada

1. The *Canadian Charter of Rights and Freedoms* guarantees the rights and freedoms set out in it subject only to such reasonable limits prescribed by law as can be demonstrably justified in a free and democratic society.

Fundamental Freedoms

Fundamental
freedoms

2. Everyone has the following fundamental freedoms:
  a) freedom of conscience and religion;
  b) freedom of thought, belief, opinion and expression, including freedom of the press and other media of communication;
  c) freedom of peaceful assembly; and
  d) freedom of association.

Democratic Rights

Democratic
rights of citizens

3. Every citizen of Canada has the right to vote in an election of members of the House of Commons or of a legislative assembly and to be qualified for membership therein.

Maximum
duration of
legislative
bodies

4. (1) No House of Commons and no legislative assembly shall continue for longer than five years from the date fixed for the return of the writs of a general election of its members.

Continuation in
special
circumstances

(2) In time of real or apprehended war, invasion or insurrection, a House of Commons may be continued by Parliament and a legislative assembly may be continued by the legislature beyond five years if such continuation is not opposed by the votes of more than one-third of the members of the House of Commons or the legislative assembly, as the case may be.

Annual sitting of
legislative
bodies

5. There shall be a sitting of Parliament and of each legislature at least once every twelve months

Mobility Rights

Mobility of
citizens

6. (1) Every citizen of Canada has the right to enter, remain in and leave Canada.

Rights to move
and gain
livelihood

(2) Every citizen of Canada and every person who has the status of a permanent resident of Canada has the right
  a) to move to and take up residence in any province; and
  b) to pursue the gaining of a livelihood in any province.

Limitation

(3) The rights specified in subsection (2) are subject to
  a) any laws or practices of general application in force in a province other than those that discriminate among persons primarily on the basis of province of present or previous residence; and
  b) any laws providing for reasonable residency requirements as a qualification for the receipt of publicly provided social services.

Affirmative

(4) Subsections (2) and (3) do not preclude any law, program or activity

action programs that has as its object the amelioration in a province of conditions of individuals in that province who are socially or economically disadvantaged if the rate of employment in that province is below the rate of employment in Canada.

Legal Rights

Life, liberty and security of person
7. Everyone has the right to life, liberty and security of the person and the right not to be deprived thereof except in accordance with the principles of fundamental justice.

Search or seizure
8. Everyone has the right to be secure against unreasonable search or seizure.

Detention or imprisonment
9. Everyone has the right not to be arbitrarily detained or imprisoned.

Arrest or detention
10. Everyone has the right on arrest or detention

a) to be informed promptly of the reasons therefor;

b) to retain and instruct counsel without delay and to be informed of that right; and

c) to have the validity of the detention determined by way of *habeas corpus* and to be released if the detention is not lawful.

Proceedings in criminal and penal matters
11. Any person charged with an offence has the right

a) to be informed without unreasonable delay of the specific offence;

b) to be tried within a reasonable time;

c) not to be compelled to be a witness in proceedings against that person in respect of the offence;

d) to be presumed innocent until proven guilty according to law in a fair and public hearing by an independent and impartial tribunal;

e) not to be denied reasonable bail without just cause;

f) except in the case of an offence under military law tried before a military tribunal, to the benefit of trial by jury where the maximum punishment for the offence is imprisonment for five years or a more severe punishment;

g) not to be found guilty on account of any act or omission unless, at the time of the act or omission, it constituted an offence under Canadian or international law or was criminal according to the general principles of law recognized by the community of nations;

h) if finally acquitted of the offence, not to be tried for it again and, if finally found guilty and punished for the offence, not to be tried or punished for it again; and

i) if found guilty of the offence and if the punishment for the offence has been varied between the time of commission and the time of sentencing, to the benefit of the lesser punishment.

Treatment or punishment

12. Everyone has the right not to be subjected to any cruel and unusual treatment or punishment.

Self-crimination

13. A witness who testifies in any proceedings has the right not to have any incriminating evidence so given used to incriminate that witness in any other proceedings, except in a prosecution for perjury or for the giving of contradictory evidence.

Interpreter

14. A party or witness in any proceedings who does not understand or speak the language in which the proceedings are conducted or who is deaf has the right to the assistance of an interpreter.

Equality Rights

Equality before and under law and equal protection and benefit of law

15. (1) Every individual is equal before and under the law and has the right to the equal protection and equal benefit of the law without discrimination and, in particular, without discrimination based on race, national or ethnic origin, colour, religion, sex, age or mental or physical disability.

Affirmative action programs

(2) Subsection (1) does not preclude any law, program or activity that has as its object the amelioration of conditions of disadvantaged individuals or groups including those that are disadvantaged because of race, national or ethnic origin, colour, religion, sex, age or mental or physical disability.

Official Languages of Canada

Official languages of Canada

16. (1) English and French are the official languages of Canada and have equality of status and equal rights and privileges as to their use in all institutions of the Parliament and government of Canada.

Official languages of New Brunswick

(2) English and French are the official languages of New Brunswick and have equality of status and equal rights and privileges as to their use in all institutions of the legislature and government of New Brunswick.

Advancement of status and use

(3) Nothing in this Charter limits the authority of Parliament or a legislature to advance the equality of status or use of English and French.

English and French linguistic communities in New Brunswick

16.1. (1) The English linguistic community and the French linguistic community in New Brunswick have equality of status and equal rights and privileges, including the right to distinct educational institutions and such distinct cultural institutions as are necessary for the preservation and promotion of those communities.

Role of the

(2) The role of the legislature and government of New Brunswick to

legislature and government of New Brunswick

preserve and promote the status, rights and privileges referred to in subsection (1) is affirmed.

Proceedings of Parliament

17. (1) Everyone has the right to use English or French in any debates and other proceedings of Parliament.

Proceedings of New Brunswick legislature

(2) Everyone has the right to use English or French in any debates and other proceedings of the legislature of New Brunswick.

Parliamentary statutes and records

18. (1) The statutes, records and journals of Parliament shall be printed and published in English and French and both language versions are equally authoritative.

New Brunswick statutes and records

(2) The statutes, records and journals of the legislature of New Brunswick shall be printed and published in English and French and both language versions are equally authoritative.

Proceedings in courts established by Parliament

19. (1) Either English or French may be used by any person in, or in any pleading in or process issuing from, any court established by Parliament.

Proceedings in New Brunswick courts

(2) Either English or French may be used by any person in, or in any pleading in or process issuing from, any court of New Brunswick.

Communications by public with federal institutions

20. (1) Any member of the public in Canada has the right to communicate with, and to receive available services from, any head or central office of an institution of the Parliament or government of Canada in English or French, and has the same right with respect to any other office of any such institution where

a) there is a significant demand for communications with and services from that office in such language; or

b) due to the nature of the office, it is reasonable that communications with and services from that office be available in both English and French.

Communications by public with New Brunswick institutions

(2) Any member of the public in New Brunswick has the right to communicate with, and to receive available services from, any office of an institution of the legislature or government of New Brunswick in English or French.

Continuation of existing constitutional provisions

21. Nothing in sections 16 to 20 abrogates or derogates from any right, privilege or obligation with respect to the English and French languages, or either of them, that exists or is continued by virtue of any other provision of the Constitution of Canada.

Rights and privileges

22. Nothing in sections 16 to 20 abrogates or derogates from any legal or

preserved

customary right or privilege acquired or enjoyed either before or after the coming into force of this Charter with respect to any language that is not English or French.

Minority Language Educational Rights

Language of instruction

23. (1) Citizens of Canada

> *a*) whose first language learned and still understood is that of the English or French linguistic minority population of the province in which they reside, or
>
> *b*) who have received their primary school instruction in Canada in English or French and reside in a province where the language in which they received that instruction is the language of the English or French linguistic minority population of the province,

have the right to have their children receive primary and secondary school instruction in that language in that province.

Continuity of language instruction

(2) Citizens of Canada of whom any child has received or is receiving primary or secondary school instruction in English or French in Canada, have the right to have all their children receive primary and secondary school instruction in the same language.

Application where numbers warrant

(3) The right of citizens of Canada under subsections (1) and (2) to have their children receive primary and secondary school instruction in the language of the English or French linguistic minority population of a province

> *a*) applies wherever in the province the number of children of citizens who have such a right is sufficient to warrant the provision to them out of public funds of minority language instruction; and
>
> *b*) includes, where the number of those children so warrants, the right to have them receive that instruction in minority language educational facilities provided out of public funds.

Enforcement

Enforcement of guaranteed rights and freedoms

24. (1) Anyone whose rights or freedoms, as guaranteed by this Charter, have been infringed or denied may apply to a court of competent jurisdiction to obtain such remedy as the court considers appropriate and just in the circumstances.

Exclusion of evidence bringing administration of justice into disrepute

(2) Where, in proceedings under subsection (1), a court concludes that evidence was obtained in a manner that infringed or denied any rights or freedoms guaranteed by this Charter, the evidence shall be excluded if it is established that, having regard to all the circumstances, the admission of it in the proceedings would bring the administration of justice into disrepute.

General

Aboriginal rights and freedoms not affected by Charter

25. The guarantee in this Charter of certain rights and freedoms shall not be construed so as to abrogate or derogate from any aboriginal, treaty or other rights or freedoms that pertain to the aboriginal peoples of Canada including

> *a*) any rights or freedoms that have been recognized by the Royal Proclamation of October 7, 1763; and
>
> *b*) any rights or freedoms that now exist by way of land claims agreements or may be so acquired.

Other rights and freedoms not affected by Charter

26. The guarantee in this Charter of certain rights and freedoms shall not be construed as denying the existence of any other rights or freedoms that exist in Canada.

Multicultural heritage

27. This Charter shall be interpreted in a manner consistent with the preservation and enhancement of the multicultural heritage of Canadians.

Rights guaranteed equally to both sexes

28. Notwithstanding anything in this Charter, the rights and freedoms referred to in it are guaranteed equally to male and female persons.

Rights respecting certain schools preserved

29. Nothing in this Charter abrogates or derogates from any rights or privileges guaranteed by or under the Constitution of Canada in respect of denominational, separate or dissentient schools.(93)

Application to territories and territorial authorities

30. A reference in this Charter to a Province or to the legislative assembly or legislature of a province shall be deemed to include a reference to the Yukon Territory and the Northwest Territories, or to the appropriate legislative authority thereof, as the case may be.

Legislative powers not extended

31. Nothing in this Charter extends the legislative powers of any body or authority.

Application of Charter

Application of Charter

32. (1)This Charter applies

> *a*) to the Parliament and government of Canada in respect of all matters within the authority of Parliament including all matters relating to the Yukon Territory and Northwest Territories; and
>
> *b*) to the legislature and government of each province in respect of all matters within the authority of the legislature of each province.

Exception

(2) Notwithstanding subsection (1), section 15 shall not have effect until three years after this section comes into force.

Exception where express declaration

33. (1) Parliament or the legislature of a province may expressly declare in an Act of Parliament or of the legislature, as the case may be, that the Act or a provision thereof shall operate notwithstanding a provision included in section 2 or sections 7 to 15 of this Charter.

Operation of exception

(2) An Act or a provision of an Act in respect of which a declaration made under this section is in effect shall have such operation as it would have but for the provision of this Charter referred to in the declaration.

Five year limitation

(3) A declaration made under subsection (1) shall cease to have effect five years after it comes into force or on such earlier date as may be specified in the declaration.

Re-enactment

(4) Parliament or the legislature of a province may re-enact a declaration made under subsection (1).

Five year limitation

(5) Subsection (3) applies in respect of a re-enactment made under subsection (4).

Citation

Citation

34. This Part may be cited as the *Canadian Charter of Rights and Freedoms.*

Appendix B

The Newfoundland and Labrador Teachers' Associations (NLTA) Code of Ethics

The Code of Professional Practice shall apply to all members and the term "teacher" as used in this code includes all members of the Newfoundland and Labrador Teachers' Association. This statement, arrived at by consensus of the Association, does not attempt to define all items of acceptable practice but rather to serve as a guide. Both individual and collective actions taken by members of any professional group may enhance or detract from the status of that profession; NLTA members are expected to be aware of this and to observe general principles of professional practice. (Note: The Code of Professional Practice shall not apply in the case of a teacher who, in good faith, provides statements or evidence to a Court of Law, an Arbitration Board, the NLTA Professional Relations Commission, the NLTA Disciplinary Committee, or any body or official duly authorized by the NLTA.)

Teacher-Pupils

(i) A teacher's first professional responsibility is to the enhancement of the quality of education provided to the pupils in his/her charge.

(ii) A teacher regards as confidential, and does not divulge, other than to appropriate persons, any information of a personal or domestic nature concerning either pupils or their homes.

(iii) A teacher keeps teaching as objective as possible in discussing with the class the controversial matters whether political, religious or racial.

(iv) A teacher does not knowingly misuse professional position for personal profit in the offering of goods or services to pupils or to their parents.

(v) A teacher does not accept pay for tutoring his/her own pupils in the subject in which that teacher gives classroom instruction.

(vi) A teacher accepts that the intellectual, moral, physical and social welfare of his/her pupils is the chief aim and end of education.

(vii) A teacher recognizes that a privileged relationship exists between the teacher and his/her pupils and shall never exploit this relationship.

(viii) A teacher who has reason to suspect that a child has suffered, or is suffering, from abuse that may have been caused or permitted by any person shall forthright report the suspected abuse to the appropriate authorities. [This section applies notwithstanding section (ii) under Teacher-Colleagues.]

Teacher-Employer

(i) A teacher does not disregard a contract, written or verbal, with a school board.

(ii) A teacher does not apply for a specific teacher's position that is not yet vacant.

(iii) A teacher does not accept a position with an employer whose relations with the Professional Organization have been declared in dispute.

Teacher-Colleagues

(i) A teacher reports through proper channels all matters harmful to the welfare of the school. S/He does not bypass immediate authority to reach higher authority without first exhausting the proper channels of communication.

(ii) A teacher does not criticize the professional competence or professional reputation of a colleague, except to proper officials and then only in confidence and after the colleague has been informed of the criticism.

(iii) A teacher notifies any other teacher whose pupils s/he proposes to tutor on a regular basis.

(iv) Teachers do not take any individual or collective action which is prejudicial to the Association, to other members of the Association, or to the profession generally.

(v) A teacher does not knowingly undermine the confidence of pupils in other teachers.

(vi) A teacher submits to the Association disputes arising from professional relationships with colleagues which cannot be resolved by personal discussion.

(vii) A teacher, before making any report on the professional competence of a colleague, provides that colleague with a copy of the report and forwards with it any written comment that the colleague chooses to make.

(viii) A teacher who is in an administrative or supervisory position makes an honest and determined effort to help and counsel another teacher before subscribing to the dismissal of that teacher.

(ix) A teacher does not actively oppose the presentation to higher authority of matters duly agreed upon by fellow teachers, except by formal minority report.

Teacher-Professional Growth

(i) A teacher acts in a manner which maintains the honor and dignity of the profession.

(ii) A teacher assists in the professional growth of colleagues through the sharing of ideas and information.

(iii) A teacher makes a constant and consistent effort to improve professionally.

Teacher-Professional Organization

(i) A teacher, or group of teachers, does not make unauthorized representation to outside bodies on behalf of the Association or its local branches.

(ii) A teacher does not refuse to follow Association directions under a legitimate job action.

(iii) A teacher adheres to collective agreements negotiated by his/her professional organization.

(iv) A teacher recognizes, as a professional responsibility, service to the Association at the local and provincial levels.

(v) A teacher who has requested representation by the Association honors commitments made on his/her behalf.

(vi) A teacher recognizes the Newfoundland and Labrador Teachers' Association as the official voice of teachers on all matters of a professional nature.

Teacher-Parents

(i) A teacher seeks to establish friendly and cooperative relationships with the home and to provide parents with information that will serve the best interests of their children.

References

Alberta School Act (2000). Edmonton: Alberta Education.

Alberta Teachers' Association (n. d.). *Code of professional conduct.* Retrieved July 26, 2007 from www.teachers.ab.ca

Anderson, J. (1992). Supervising students at recess. *Canadian School Executive, 11*(9), 33-34.

Association of American Educators (sss). *Code of ethics.* Retrieved July 10, 2007 from www.aaeteachers.org/code-ethics.shtml

Barnhorst, R. (2004). The Youth Criminal Justice Act: New directions and implementation issues. *The Journal of Criminology and Criminal Justice. 46*(3), 231-250.

Bezeau, L. M. (1995). *Educational administration for Canadian teachers.* Toronto: Copp Clark.

Black-Branch, J. L. (1997). *Rights and realities: The judicial impact of the Canadian Charter of Rights and Freedoms on education, case law and political jurisprudence.* Brookfield, VT: Ashgate.

Brown, A. F. (1998). *Legal handbook for educators* (4th ed.). Scarborough, ON: Thomson Canada.

Brown, A. F. & Zuker, M. A. (2002). *Education law* (3rd. ed.). Toronto: Thomson Carswell.

Caldwell, B. J., & Spinks, J. M. (1988). *The self-managing school.* Philadelphia: Falmer.

Callahan, B. (2004, December 16). Board liable for teacher's assault. *The Telegram.*

Canadian Intellectual Property Office (2007). *A guide to copyrights: Copyright protection.* Ottawa: Government of Canada. Retrieved May 15, 2007 from strategis.ic.gc.ca/sc_mrksv/cipo/cp/cp_circ_12-e.html

Canadian Unity Information Office (1984). *The charter of rights and freedoms.* Ottawa: Minister of Supply and Services Canada.

Carrington, P. J. & Schulenberg, J. L. (2004). Introduction: The Youth Criminal Justice Act – A new era in Canadian juvenile justice? *The Journal of Criminology and Criminal Justice, 46*(3), 219-223.

Carrington, P. J., & Schulenberg, J. L. (2005). *The impact of the Youth Criminal Justice Act on police charging practices with young persons: A preliminary statistical assessment.* Retrieved April 15, 2007, from www.justice.gc.ca/en/ps/yj/research/pcarrington-jschulenberg//pdf/Carrington-schulenberg-assessment.pdf

Coombs, C. (2005). Intimidation. . . why it works and how to overcome it. *The Newfoundland and Labrador Teachers' Association Bulletin, 48*(7), 18.

Criminal Code of Canada – Section 43 (1985). Retrieved January 17, 2007 from www.canlii.org/ca/sta/c-46/sec43.html

Criminal Code of Canada – Sections 151, 152, & 153 (1985). Retrieved January 21, 2007 from www.canlii.org/ca/sta/c-46/sec153.1.html

Criminal Code of Canada – Section 217.1 (2004). Retrieved July 23, 2007 from laws.justice.gc.ca/en/ShowDoc/cs/c-46///en?page=1

Cunningham, G. (1963). Policy and practice. *Public Administration, 41,* 229-238.

Department of Justice (1985). *The Criminal Code of Canada.* Ottawa: Author. Retrieved May 15, 2007 from laws.justice.gc.ca/en/ShowDoc/cs/c-46///-/en?page=1

Dickinson, G. M. & MacKay, A. W. (1989). *Rights, freedoms, and the education system in Canada: Cases and materials.* Toronto: Emond-Montgomery.

Doctor, E. (1999, April). Someone else's nightmare: Sexual misconduct in schools. Paper presented at the annual meeting of the Canadian Association for the Practical Study of Law in Education, Toronto, ON.

Dougherty, J. W. (2004). *Torts and liability: An educator's short guide.* Bloomington, IN: Phi Delta Kappa Educational Foundation.

Dove, M. K., Miller, K. L., & Miller, S. M. (2003). Reporting suspected child abuse: An educator's legal, ethical and moral obligation. *Delta Kappa Gamma Bulletin, 69*(3), 21-26.

Duke, D. L., & Canady, R. L. (1991). *School policy.* New York: McGraw-Hill.

Edmonton School District No. 7 Teachers' Collective Agreement (2003-2006). Edmonton: Alberta Teachers' Association.

Fullan, M. (2001). *The new meaning of educational change* (3rd ed.). New York: Teachers College.

Harris, L. E. (2001). *Canadian copyright law* (3rd. ed.). Toronto: McGraw-Hill.

Harris, P., Weagant, B., Cole, D., & Weinper, F. (2004). Working in the trenches with the YCJA. *The Journal of Criminology and Criminal Justice, 46*(3), 367-389.

Hoy, W. K., & Miskel, C. G. (2001). *Educational administration: Theory, research, and practice* (6th ed.). New York: McGraw-Hill.

Hoyle, E. (1986). *The politics of school management.* London: Hodder and Stroughton.

Hurlbert, M. A., & Hurlbert, E. L. (1992). *School law under the Charter of Rights and Freedoms.* Calgary: University of Calgary.

Imbrogno, A. (2000). Corporal punishment in America's public schools and the U. N. Convention on the rights of the child: A case for non-ratification. *Journal of Law and Education, 29*(2), 125-146.

James, S., & DeVaney, S. (1994). Reporting suspected sexual abuse: A study of counselor and counselor trainee responses. *Elementary School Guidance & Counseling, 28,* 257-263.

Keel, R. G. (1998). *Student rights and responsibilities: Attendance and discipline.* Toronto: Emond Montgomery.

Kenny, M. C. (2001). Child abuse reporting: Teachers' perceived deterrents. *Child Abuse & Neglect, 25*(1), 81-92.

Kitchen, J. & Corbett, R. (1995). *Negligence and liability: A guide for recreation and sport organizations.* Edmonton, AB: Centre for Sport and Law.

LaMorte, M. W. (1999). *School law: Cases and concepts* (6th ed.). Needham Heights, MA: Allyn and Bacon.

Levin, J., Nolan, J. F., Kerr, J. W., & Elliott, A. E. (2004). *Principles of classroom management: A professional decision-making model.* Toronto: Pearson.

Luffman, Jacqueline (1997). A profile of home schooling in Canada. *Education Quarterly Review, 1997.* Statistics Canada Catalog 81-003-XPB, Vol. 4, no. 4.

MacKay, A. W. (1984). *Education law in Canada.* Toronto: Emond Montgomery.

MacKay, A. W. & Flood, T. L. (2001). Negligence principles in the school context: New challenges for the "careful parent." *Education and Law Journal, 14*(X), 137-165.

MacKay, A. W., & Sutherland, L. I. (1992). *Teachers and the law: A practical guide for educators.* Toronto: Emond Montgomery.

MacKay, A. W., & Sutherland, L. I. (2006). *Teachers and the law: A practical guide for educators* (2nd ed.). Toronto: Emond Montgomery.

MacLarkey, W. R. (2004). Amendments to Criminal Code impose criminal liability for unsafe workplaces. *Capsle COMMENTS, 13*(4), 3 - 5.

Manitoba Workplace Safety and Health Act (2007). Retrieved July 25, 2007 from www.canlii.org

McEwen, N. (1995). Accountability in education in Canada. *Canadian Journal of Education, 20*(1), 1-17.

McGreal, T. L. (1983). *Successful teacher evaluation.* Alexandria, VA: Association for Supervision and Curriculum Development.

Murao v. Blackcomb Skiing Enterprises Limited Partnership (2003). Retrieved July 30, 2007 from www.canlii.org/eliisa/highlight.do?text=Murao+v.+-Blackcomb+Skiing+Enterprises+Limited+Partners

New Brunswick Education Act (1997). Fredericton: Department of Education.

New Brunswick Teachers' Federation Collective Agreement (September 1, 2000 to February 29, 2004). Fredericton: New Brunswick Teachers' Federation.

Newfoundland and Labrador Occupational Health and Safety Act (1990). Retrieved July 25, 2007 from www.canlii.org

Newfoundland and Labrador Schools Act (1997). St. John's: Department of Education.

Newfoundland and Labrador Teachers' Association (n.d.). *Code of ethics.* Retrieved July 20, 2007 from www.nlta.nl.ca

Newfoundland and Labrador Teachers' Association Collective Agreement September 1, 2001 – August 31, 2004). Retrieved July 20, 2007 from www.nlta.nl.ca

Noel, W. (2005). *Copyright matters* (2nd ed.). Ottawa: Council of Ministers of Education.

Northwest Territories Teachers' Association (n. d.). *Code of ethics.* Retrieved July 18, 2007 from www.nwtta.nt.ca

Nova Scotia Education Act (1996). Halifax: Department of Education.

Nova Scotia Teachers' Union (n. d.). *Code of ethics.* Retrieved July 25, 2007 from www.nstu.ca

Nova Scotia Teachers' Union Collective Agreement (2002-2005). Halifax: Nova Scotia Teachers' Union.

Ontario College of Teachers (n. d.). Ontario College. *The ethical standards for the teaching profession.* Toronto: Author.

Ontario Education Act (1990). Toronto: Ministry of Education.

Ontario Principals' Council (2004). OPC Youth Criminal Justice Act Symposium. *CAPSLE Comments, 13*(4).

O'Toole, R., Webster, S. W., O'Toole, A. W. & Lucal, B. (1999). Mandatory reporting: A policy without reason. *Child Abuse & Neglect, 28*(12), 1083-1101.

Payne, N. A. (2006). The Youth Criminal Justice Act: Necessary change or political expediency. Unpublished honors thesis, Memorial University of Newfoundland, St. John's, NL.

Platt, P. (1991). *A police guide to the Young Offenders Act.* Toronto: Butterworths.

Pulis, J. E., & Sprott, J. B. (2005). Probation sentences and proportionality under the Young Offenders Act and the Youth Criminal Justice Act. *The Journal of Criminology and Criminal Justice, 47*(4), 709-723.

Prince Edward Island School Act (1988). Charlottetown: Government of Prince Edward Island.

Prince Edward Island Child Protection Act (1988). Charlottetown: Government of Prince Edward Island.

Quebec Education Act (2005). Quebec City: Ministry of Education.

Richter, I. (1994). Law and administration in education. In T. Husen & T. N. Postlethwaite (Eds.), *The international encyclopedia of education* (2nd ed.). Oxford: Pergamon.

Saskatchewan Education Act (1995). Regina: Department of Education.,

Saskatchewan Teachers' Federation (n. d.). Code of ethics. Retrieved July 21, 2007 from www.stf.sk.ca

Sergiovanni, T. J. (1995). *The principalship: A reflective practice perspective* (3rd ed.). Boston: Allyn and Bacon.

Sergiovanni, T. J., Burlingame, M., Coombs, F. S., & Thurston, P. W. (1999). *Educational governance and administration* (4th ed.). Needham Heights, MA: Allyn & Bacon.

Shariff, S. (2004). Travel and terror: Re-allocating, minimizing and managing risks of foreign excursions and outdoor education field trips. *Education and Law Journal, 14*(2), 137-165.

Smith, D. (1996). Parent-generated home study in Canada. *The Canadian School Executive, 15*(8), 9-1.

Strauss, M. A., & Donnelly, D. A. (1993). Corporal punishment of adolescents by American parents. *Youth and Society, 24*(4), 419-442.

Strike, K. A., & Soltis, J. F. (1992). *The ethics of teaching* (2nd ed.). New York: Teachers College.

Supreme Court of Canada (1998). *R. v. M. (M. R.).* Retrieved April 20, 2007 from www.canlii.org/ca/cas/scc/1998/1998scc84.html p. 4

Supreme Court of Canada (2004). *Canadian Foundation for Children, Youth and the Law v. Attorney General in Right of Canada.* Retrieved January 20, 2007 from www.canlii.org/ca/cas/scc/2004/2004scc4.html

Sydor, S. (2006). Teacher education needs more education law. *Proceedings of the Seventeenth Annual Conference of the Canadian Association for the Practical study of Law in Education,* Montreal, Canada, 2, 927-936.

Tustin, L., & Lutes, R. E. (2004). *A guide to the Youth Criminal Justice Act.* Markham, ON: LexisNexis Canada.

Watkinson, A. M. (1999). *Education, student rights and the Charter.* Saskatoon, SK: Purich.

Weir, R. W. (2003, June). What the new Youth Criminal Justice Act means to your school. *Capsle COMMENTS, 12*(4), 1-3.

Winnipeg Teachers' Association Collective Agreement (July 1, 2003 – June 30, 2005). Winnipeg: Winnipeg Teachers' Association.

Yogis, J. A. (1995). *Canadian law dictionary* (3rd. ed.). Hauppauge, NY: Barron's.

Young, J. & Levin, B. (2002). *Understanding Canadian schools: An introduction to educational administration* (3rd ed.). Scarborough, ON: Thomson Nelson.

Index